200 twenty-minute meals

hamlyn | all color cookbook

200 twenty-minute meals

An Hachette UK company
www.hachette.co.uk

First published in Great Britain in 2011 by Hamlyn
a division of Octopus Publishing Group Ltd
Endeavour House, 189 Shaftesbury Avenue
London WC2H 8JY
www.octopusbooks.co.uk

Distributed in the US and Canada by
Hachette Book Group USA, 237 Park Avenue
New York, NY 10017 USA

Copyright © Octopus Publishing Group Ltd 2011
Some of the recipes in this book have previously appeared
in other books published by Hamlyn.

ISBN: 978 0 60062 341 0
A CIP catalog record for this book is available
from the British Library
Printed and bound in China
1 2 3 4 5 6 7 8 9 10

Standard level spoon measurements are used in all recipes.

Ovens should be preheated to the specified temperature.
If using a fan-assisted oven, follow the manufacturer's
instructions for adjusting the time and the temperature.

Fresh herbs should be used unless otherwise stated.
Medium eggs should be used unless otherwise stated.

Poultry should be cooked thoroughly. To test if poultry is
cooked, pierce the flesh through the thickest part with a
skewer or fork—the juices should run clear, never pink or red.

People with known nut allergies should avoid recipes
containing nuts or nut derivatives, and vulnerable people
should avoid dishes containing raw or lightly cooked eggs.

contents

introduction

introduction

It is 7:30 P.M., your train was late, it is getting dark outside, the dishwasher still needs emptying, and you are starving. These are not the best circumstances in which to start cooking a meal, but let's face it, it is the reality of most Mondays, Tuesdays, Wednesdays, and Thursdays. In fact, if we'd had the space on the cover, we might well have called this book, "The Monday-to-Thursday Meal Book" because it is on those days that we tend to find ourselves throwing together meals in a matter of minutes. If we can't cook something tasty in less than 20 minutes, most of us end up getting a ready-meal out of the freezer and slipping it guiltily into the microwave, or closing the cupboards, and ordering a takeout.

In this small but useful book, we have a clear message for you. Save your money! Don't order that takeout! In the time it would take

you to heat up a ready-meal in the oven, you can make a delicious, nutritious, home-cooked supper and, more often than not, for less than it would have cost you for that ready-meal. All you need are some key cupboard ingredients, some vital pieces of kitchen equipment, and a little bit of meal planning.

the art of meal planning

For those of us who are working all day, either looking after children in the home or in paid work outside the home, finding the time to sit down and plan meals seems just about impossible. But by doing so, the next time you find yourself with a growling stomach staring into an empty fridge at 7:30 P.M., all you have to do is look at your meal list and find the ingredients. We promise you that 20 minutes or so later you will be sitting down to a tasty home-cooked supper. It couldn't be simpler. So, after you have eaten tonight, instead of turning on the TV or the computer, spend a few minutes going through this book. Pick out four or five meals that appeal to you and then turn on the computer and use it to place your internet grocery order. Keep your meal list on the fridge door and put a tick next to the meals as you cook them. It sounds obvious, but such a small, simple task means you or your partner will know what food has been bought for what meal; it means less wasted food; time saved shopping for extra ingredients (which

have been used up unknowingly on another meal); and it saves you the bother of having to decide what to cook.

So which meals should you choose when planning your suppers? First, keep in mind your and your family's tastes and, where possible, combine your and their favorites with some new foods. Second, factor in your budget. Third, remember nutrition.

busy people need good nutrition

When it comes to ensuring that you are getting a balanced, nutritious diet, our suggestion is that you include as many · different types of food through the course of the week as is economical and practical. Doing this means you are taking in a whole range of nutrients and also that you won't get bored cooking the same meals all the time. It also means that—if you're cooking for a

family—everyone gets to have their favorite food at least once a week.

Fruit and vegetables are enormously important to your overall health and vitality and should take up at least one-third of your dinner plate. They are packed with important vitamins and minerals, such as iron, potassium, zinc, and calcium, which help your mind and body function well. When your life is busy and stressful, fruits and vegetables are even more important in your diet because they are excellent sources of antioxidants, which help ward off illness.

Remembering all the nutritional benefits of long lists of foods is practically impossible, so try and follow this simple rule. Every day, eat some orange and red fruits and vegetables, such as red bell peppers, tomatoes, radishes, apricots, carrots, oranges, and squashes, and some dark green vegetables, such as broccoli,

broccoli raab, chard, and spinach, and herbs, like parsley, to benefit from their high levels of vitamins and antioxidants. Remember: the fresher your fruit and vegetables are, the higher their nutritional value.

You will notice as you look through this book that many of the recipes involve steaming or stir-frying vegetables. We have included these recipes not only because these methods save time and are efficient, but also because heat destroys the vitamins. Keeping the cooking time to a minimum improves the levels of nutrition in your meals.

Protein should make up another third of your dinner plate. Mixing up the protein sources in your diet will ensure you benefit from a wide range of nutrients. Gone are the days when meat was heralded as the first-class protein and all other forms of protein were considered second class. These days it is recommended that, as well as some red meat and poultry, we should include a range of omega-rich fish and seafood in our diets (ideally at least twice a week) as well as plenty of nuts and seeds, some low-fat dairy products, such as cheese, milk, and yogurt, some eggs and, of course, plenty of legumes. When choosing your protein, remember that weight for weight, beans contain almost as much protein as a steak—at a fraction of the cost—and with many more health benefits. Beans are rich in various health-promoting minerals, and they help protect against cardiovascular diseases, osteoporosis, and various cancers. Remember, too, that they also have a low GI, which means they provide slow-release energy, an important factor for diabetics. For the sake of speed, you can use canned beans in the recipes in this book, as opposed to dried beans, which need soaking overnight and then boiling.

Complex carbohydrates should make up the remaining third of your plate and should form the basis of your diet. Complex carbohydrates are vital sources of fiber and also give our cells the energy they need. That's why when we get in from work at 7 P.M. and haven't eaten since lunchtime, we often reach for the complex carbohydrates for our first "food fix"—our bodies (and brains!) know that we are lacking glucose and need immediate

energy. Complex carbohydrates do not refer exclusively to whole grains, such as oats and brown rice, or bread and pasta. They also include potatoes and other starchy vegetables, such as sweet potatoes, corn, and even bell peppers and tomatoes. Many of the recipes in this book use a wide range of delicious vegetables, and these will give you a burst of flavor, and a good helping of energy and fiber.

Once you have chosen your meals, go shopping for the fresh ingredients and any other specific ingredients that you don't have. Why not take a look at our recommended cupboard ingredient list (see page 13). By keeping these foods in your kitchen cupboards all the time, you will be able to whip up an exciting meal even on days when you're weren't expecting to have to cook.

what ingredients should you always have available?

Most fresh produce, such as meat, poultry, fish, fruit, and vegetables, should ideally be bought as fresh as possible and with specific meals in mind to reduce waste. However, there are some fresh ingredients that you can always have in your fridge and freezer no matter what kind of meal you are planning to cook because they are always useful to have available for a wide variety of different recipes.

In the freezer, keep fresh ginger root in resealable freezer bags and grate it straight into the pan from frozen. Fresh chilies can also be frozen in freezer bags and need only a few minutes on a plate to thaw out before they are soft enough to chop. It is possible to freeze certain fresh herbs for use in case of emergencies, though be aware that they do lose some of their flavor and pungency when frozen. Most bread products, including store-bought pizza bases, naans, and pita breads, can be kept in the freezer and cooked straight from frozen, or defrosted in the microwave for a few seconds just before cooking.

In the fridge we recommend keeping a tub of crème fraîche (or sour cream), a small carton of heavy cream, butter, eggs, Cheddar and Parmesan cheese, and a carton of plain natural yogurt. All these foodstuffs can be used in various recipes in this book and are bound to come in useful before they reach their use-by date.

For your kitchen cupboards, we would recommend you stock up on the following:

- Cans or tubes of tomato paste and bottles or cans of tomato purée
- Canned diced or chopped tomatoes
- A selection of canned legumes, including chickpeas
- A selection of canned vegetables
- A jar of pitted black olives in brine
- Some canned fish—salmon or tuna
- Stock cubes, including vegetable, chicken, fish, and beef or lamb
- Dried herbs and spices, including ground cumin, ground coriander seed, cinnamon, Chinese five-spice powder, saffron, mixed herbs, mixed spice, and ground nutmeg
- Jars of ginger, lemongrass, and garlic paste (incredible time-savers with very little compromise in flavor)

- Bottled oils, including olive, peanut, and sesame oils
- Dark and light soy sauce
- Sweet chili sauce
- Worcestershire sauce
- Salt and pepper
- Vinegar, including balsamic and white wine vinegar
- Mustard seeds and a jar of Dijon mustard
- Dried chili flakes
- Dried pasta and noodles
- Brown and white rice (brown rice is better for you, but takes an extra 10 minutes to cook)
- Fish sauce
- Cashews, almonds, and peanuts (stored in airtight containers) are extremely useful
- Lime leaves
- Coconut milk
- All-purpose, self-rising flour and cornstarch

essential kitchen equipment

Making good food quickly is something you will get better at with practice, but ultimately certain items of equipment are invaluable for getting together a really tasty meal in a matter of minutes. Essential items include a combination of different-sized, good-quality saucepans and a skillet, complete with lids, a colander and a fine-mesh sieve, and at least two good-sized baking pans. Standard kitchen utensils include a slotted spoon, a metal spatula or lifter, a potato masher, tongs, rubber scrapers, vegetable peelers, a whisk, some

mixing bowls, and liquid measuring cups, as well as some good-quality kitchen knives. You would also benefit from having:

• A food processor with various attachments, including a whisk and beater, slicer disks, and a standard cutting blade. Even though it is possible to chop, grate, slice, knead, and mix everything by hand, a food processor does all these things very quickly and efficiently and saves you time and energy. It is a vital piece of equipment for the busy, time-impoverished cook.
• A blender, which can blend or chop foods almost instantly and can also pulverize ingredients, so is excellent for making soup.
• A garlic crusher takes seconds to give a great garlic taste as opposed to minutes.
• A two- or ideally three-level steamer pan.
• A box grater is much easier and therefore quicker to use then a single-sided grater.
• A microwave for defrosting and cooking certain foods while others are being cooked on the stove.

make your kitchen space work for you

You may have all the key ingredients in your cupboards and a whole range of delicious food in the fridge, but when you get down to the job of actually cooking your meal, you need to have a workspace that works for you.

Reclaim any space in your kitchen that is taken up with noncooking items—you need every bit of space to house the equipment

be ready to serve

Finally, when you are ready to serve your meal, remember that clearing the table and setting it at the last second only adds to tension and means your culinary efforts will be left on the side going cold while you deal with the chaos in the dining area. If you are eating with your family or friends, ask them to clear the table and set it while you cook. This is a very good habit for children to get into and, for friends, it is a small gesture of thanks for the meal you have cooked for them.

Everyone is seated, conversation is flowing, and the food has been served. Now all there is to do is enjoy the meal you have prepared and revel in the fact that you have made this plate of magic in less time than it would have taken to go get that takeout and bring it back. Some of the best things in life are the quickest and simplest. Savor and enjoy!

and utensils that you need to prepare a meal in the least amount of time possible. Look inside your kitchen drawers and ensure they are uncluttered. You can put large utensils like ladles, spatulas, whisks, and wooden spoons in a crock next to the stove within easy reach. Now think about where you store the kitchen equipment you use the most. Your mixing bowls, grater, garlic crusher, food processor, and measuring cups and spoons, not to mention your collection of sharpened knives, should be easy to reach, not crammed into the back of a drawer or stuck behind a stack of heavy dishes. It sounds obvious, but you'd be surprised how habit leads us to keep essential equipment in places they've been for years, but that cause us stress and waste our time when cooking. It may take an hour or so one weekend, but getting your kitchen organized will really help you in your mission to make quick, delicious meals on a regular basis.

snacks & light bites

garlic & bean pâté

Serves **4**

Preparation time **5 minutes**

14 oz can **flageolet beans**, drained

½ cup **cream cheese**

2 **garlic cloves**, chopped

3 tablespoons **pesto**

2 **scallions**, chopped

1 tablespoon **olive oil**

salt and **pepper**

To serve

cucumber sticks

4 **pita bread**

Put the beans, cream cheese, garlic, and 2 tablespoons of the pesto in a food processor or blender and blend until smooth.

Add the scallions and salt and pepper to taste and blend for 10 seconds. Spoon into a dish and chill until required. Mix the remaining pesto with the olive oil and drizzle on top before serving with cucumber sticks and pita bread lightly toasted and cut into thick strips.

For hummus & feta dip, drain a 14 oz can of chickpeas and pour them into a food processor with 3 tablespoons tahini paste, 3 tablespoons lemon juice, ¼ cup water, ½ teaspoon ground cumin, 1 crushed garlic clove, and salt and pepper and whizz until combined. With the motor still running, pour 2 tablespoons olive oil through the feed tube in a thin, steady stream and process until smooth. Spoon into a serving dish and sprinkle ⅔ cup feta cheese over the top. Serve with raw vegetable sticks or toasted pita bread.

egg pots with smoked salmon

Serves **4**
Preparation time **5 minutes**
Cooking time **10–15 minutes**

7 oz **smoked salmon
trimmings**
2 tablespoons chopped
chives
4 **eggs**
4 tablespoons **heavy cream**
pepper

To serve
4 slices **bread**

Divide the smoked salmon and chives among
4 buttered ramekins. Make a small indentation in the
salmon with the back of a spoon and break an egg
into the hollow, sprinkle with a little pepper, and spoon
the cream over the top.

Put the ramekins in a roasting pan and half-fill the pan
with boiling water. Bake in a preheated oven, 350°F, for
10–15 minutes or until the eggs have just set.

Remove from the oven and leave to cool for a few
minutes, then serve with toasted bread.

For egg pots with mushrooms & thyme, heat about
2 teaspoons of butter in a skillet, add 1 small, finely
chopped onion, and fry gently until softened. Add
2 cups chopped mushrooms and the leaves from a
sprig of thyme and cook until the excess liquid has
evaporated. Season with salt and pepper and a few
gratings of fresh nutmeg. Divide the mixture among the
4 buttered ramekins, break an egg into each, and then
spoon the cream on top. Cook as above and serve with
toasted bread.

peppered chicken skewers

Serves **4**
Preparation time **10 minutes**,
    plus marinating
Cooking time **10 minutes**

4 boneless, skinless **chicken
    breasts**, about 5 oz each
2 tablespoons finely chopped
    rosemary, plus extra to
    garnish
2 **garlic cloves**, finely chopped
3 tablespoons **lemon juice**
2 teaspoons **mustard**
1 tablespoon **liquid honey**
2 teaspoons freshly ground
    black pepper
1 tablespoon **olive oil**
pinch of **salt**

To serve
lemon wedges

Lay a chicken breast between 2 sheets of plastic wrap
and flatten slightly with a rolling pin. Repeat with the
remaining chicken breasts, then cut the chicken into
thick strips.

Put the chicken strips in a nonmetallic bowl and add the
remaining ingredients. Mix well, then cover and leave to
marinate in the refrigerator for 5–10 minutes.

Thread the chicken strips onto 8 skewers and cook
under a preheated medium-hot broiler for 4–5 minutes
on each side or until the chicken is cooked through.
Garnish with rosemary, and serve immediately with
lemon wedges.

For beef & sweet chili sesame skewers, slice
1½ lb trimmed sirloin or round steak into long, thick
strips. Place in a small bowl, drizzle with olive oil, and
season with salt and pepper. Thread onto skewers and
cook under a preheated hot broiler for 1 minute on each
side. Remove from the heat and coat the skewers with
2 tablespoons sweet chili sauce and sprinkle with
sesame seeds. Cook under the broiler for a further
minute on each side or until glazed and cooked through.
Serve with a green salad.

mozzarella & tomato ciabatta

Serves **2**
Preparation time **5 minutes**
Cooking time **12 minutes**

2 small, single-serving
 ciabatta loaves
2 oz **mozzarella cheese**
2 large **tomatoes**
1 large or 2 small **avocados**
1 tablespoon roughly
 chopped **basil**
pepper

Put the ciabatta loaves on a cookie sheet and warm in a preheated oven, 350°F, for about 10 minutes.

Meanwhile, thinly slice the mozzarella and slice the tomatoes. Halve, stone, peel, and slice the avocados.

Remove the ciabatta loaves from the oven and cut each one in half. Layer the avocado, mozzarella, and tomato slices on the 2 bottom halves, add the basil, and sprinkle with pepper. Return the bottom halves with the filling to the oven for 2–3 minutes or until the mozzarella has melted. Put the top halves on top and serve immediately.

For pesto, mozzarella & roasted bell pepper ciabatta, bake and halve 2 ciabatta loaves as above. Spread 1 teaspoon pesto over the bottom halves of each ciabatta loaf, and layer with the mozzarella and a few drained roasted bell peppers from a jar. Omit the avocado and tomato, add the basil, and season. Cook in the oven, as above.

peanut, pomelo & shrimp salad

Serves **4**
Preparation time **15 minutes**
Cooking time **1–2 minutes**

1 large **pomelo**
1 scant cup **unsalted peanuts**, toasted and roughly chopped
6 oz raw peeled **jumbo shrimp**
4 **scallions**
6 **mint leaves**
2 tablespoons **grapefruit juice**
½ tablespoon **Thai fish sauce**
1 large **red chili**, seeded and finely sliced
pinch of crushed **dried chilies** or **black pepper**
pinch of grated fresh **nutmeg**

Cut the pomelo in half and scoop out the segments and juice. Discard the pith and thick skin surrounding each segment and break the flesh into small pieces. Put the flesh into a large bowl and stir in the peanuts. Set aside to allow the flavors to blend.

Poach the shrimp in a saucepan of simmering water for 1–2 minutes or until they turn pink and are cooked through. Remove with a slotted spoon and drain well.

While the shrimp are cooling, finely shred the scallions and mint leaves.

Add the shrimp to the pomelo flesh with the grapefruit juice, fish sauce, scallions, and mint. Sprinkle the red chili, crushed dried chilies or pepper, and freshly grated nutmeg over the salad and toss together, and serve.

For pomelo & shrimp salad with vermicelli noodles, put 5 oz vermicelli noodles in a large heatproof bowl, pour over boiling water to cover and leave to stand for 5 minutes or according to the instructions on the package, until tender. Meanwhile, whisk together the juice of 1 lime, 1 tablespoon sweet chili sauce, and 1 teaspoon Thai fish sauce in a bowl. Drain the noodles and pour the dressing over them. Toss well to combine. Prepare the rest of the salad as above. Toss all the ingredients together, garnish with peanuts and roughly chopped herbs, and serve immediately.

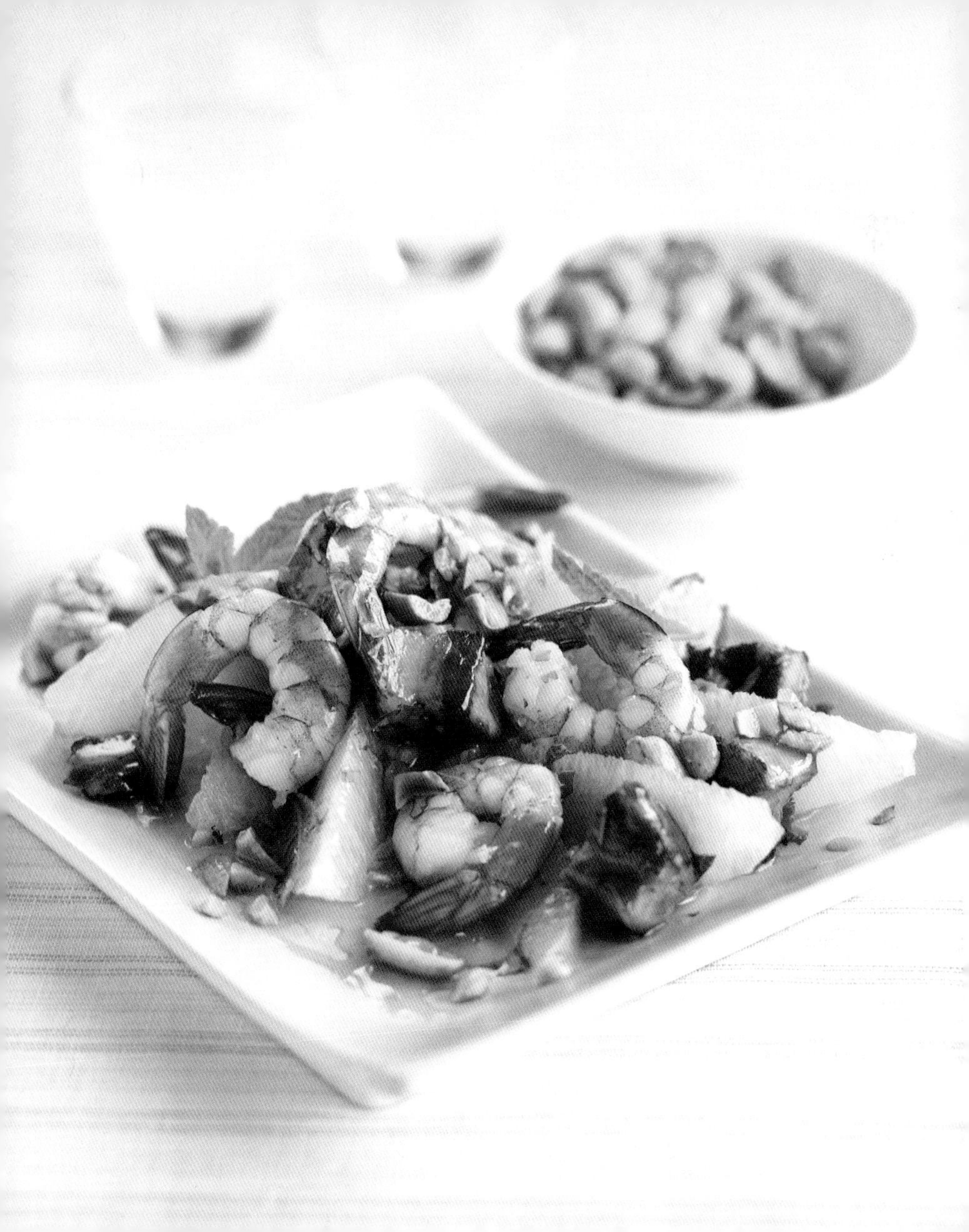

chili thai beef baguettes

Serves **4**
Preparation time **5 minutes**
Cooking time **4 minutes**

1 lb thick **sirloin steak,**
  trimmed
1 tablespoon **olive oil**
4 small baguettes
4 sprigs of **cilantro**
4 sprigs of **Thai** or **ordinary**
  basil
4 sprigs of **mint**
salt and **pepper**

Dressing
2 tablespoons **Thai fish sauce**
2 tablespoons **lime juice**
2 tablespoons **soft light**
  brown sugar
1 large **red chili,** seeded and
  thinly sliced

Brush the steak with the oil and season well with salt and pepper. Heat a ridged griddle pan until very hot, add the steak, and cook over high heat for 2 minutes on each side or until seared all over. The steak should be rare. Remove from the pan and leave to rest for 5 minutes, then cut into thin slices.

While the steak is resting, make the dressing. Mix together the fish sauce, lime juice, and sugar in a bowl and stir in the chili until the sugar has dissolved.

Split the baguettes in half lengthwise and fill with the herbs, beef slices, and any juices. Pour the dressing carefully over, season, and serve.

For Thai beef salad, cook, rest, and slice the steak, as above. Toss with 1 sliced Lebanese cucumber (or a small seedless cucumber), 1¾ cups halved cherry tomatoes, 1 cup bean sprouts, and a handful each of Thai or ordinary basil, fresh cilantro, and mint leaves in a bowl. Mix together the juice of ½ lime, 1 teaspoon sesame oil, 1 teaspoon superfine sugar, 1 teaspoon Thai fish sauce, and 1 tablespoon peanut oil in a bowl. Add to the salad, toss well until coated, and serve.

aromatic chicken pancakes

Serves **4**
Preparation time **10 minutes**
Cooking time **7 minutes**

4 boneless, skinless **chicken breasts**, about 5 oz each
6 tablespoons **hoisin sauce**

To serve
12 **Chinese pancakes**
½ **cucumber**, cut into matchsticks
12 **scallions**, thinly sliced
handful of **cilantro leaves**
4 tablespoons **hoisin sauce** mixed with 3 tablespoons **water**

Lay a chicken breast between 2 sheets of plastic wrap and flatten with a rolling pin until it is 1 inch thick. Repeat with the remaining chicken breasts. Transfer to a baking pan and brush with some of the hoisin sauce.

Cook the chicken breasts under a preheated hot broiler for 4 minutes. Turn them over, brush with the remaining hoisin sauce, and cook for a further 3 minutes or until the chicken is cooked through.

Meanwhile, warm the pancakes in a bamboo steamer for 3 minutes or until heated through.

Slice the chicken thinly and arrange it on a serving plate. Serve with the pancakes, accompanied by the cucumber, scallions, cilantro, and diluted hoisin sauce in separate bowls, so that everyone can assemble their own pancakes.

For satay chicken pancakes, in a nonmetallic bowl, mix together 6 tablespoons dark soy sauce, 2 tablespoons sesame oil, and 1 teaspoon Chinese five-spice powder. Add the flattened chicken breasts, and coat evenly with the marinade. Cover and leave to marinate in the refrigerator. Put 4 tablespoons peanut butter, 1 tablespoon dark soy sauce, ½ teaspoon cumin powder, ½ teaspoon ground coriander seed, a pinch of paprika, and ½ cup water in a saucepan and mix together over low heat. Transfer to 4 small bowls. Cook the chicken and pancakes as above and serve with the satay sauce.

rösti potatoes with ham & eggs

Serves **2**
Preparation time **10 minutes**
Cooking time **10–12 minutes**

1 lb round white or round red
   potatoes, peeled
2 tablespoons **butter**
2 **eggs**
2 slices of **smoked ham**
salt and **pepper**

To serve
tomato ketchup

Grate the potatoes using a box grater and place on a clean tea towel. Wrapping them in the towel, squeeze out all the excess moisture, transfer to a bowl, and season to taste with salt and pepper.

Melt the butter in a large nonstick skillet. Divide the potato mixture into quarters and form each into a 4-inch cake. Add to the skillet and cook over medium heat for 5–6 minutes on each side or until lightly golden and cooked through.

Meanwhile, poach or fry the eggs. Serve 2 rösti potatoes per person, topped with an egg, with a slice of smoked ham and some tomato ketchup, if liked.

For sweet potato rösti with egg & spinach, grate 8 oz sweet potatoes and 8 oz round white or round red potatoes as above and combine. Make and cook the rösti potatoes as above. Serve 2 rösti potatoes per person, topped with a poached egg and a small handful of baby spinach leaves.

broiled goat cheese with salsa

Serves **4**
Preparation time: **10 minutes**
Cooking time **3–5 minutes**

8 slices **ciabatta** or **French
baguette**
1 tablespoon finely chopped
rosemary
½ teaspoon freshly ground
red or **black pepper**
5 oz cylindrical piece of **goat
cheese**, about 2 inches
across
a little beaten **egg white**

Salsa
3½ oz **piquillo peppers** from
a jar, drained
1 **scallion**, finely chopped
1 tablespoon **lime juice**
2 teaspoons **superfine sugar**

Toast the ciabatta or French baguette slices lightly on both sides and set aside on a serving plate.

Make the salsa by slicing the peppers as thinly as possible, then mix with the scallion, lime juice, and sugar in a bowl.

Brush a foil-lined broiler pan lightly with oil. Mix together the rosemary and ground pepper on a plate.

Brush the rind of the cheese in egg white, then roll it in the rosemary and pepper mixture. Cut the cheese horizontally into 8 slices, each ½ inch thick, and place them on the foil.

Cook under a preheated broiler until the cheese begins to bubble and slightly turn golden. Top the ciabatta slices with a spoonful of salsa, then slide a slice of cooked cheese on top of each and serve immediately.

For broiled haloumi & olive tapenade, replace the goat cheese with 5 oz haloumi cheese, cut into ½ inch slices. Omit the rosemary and ground pepper mixture. Coat the haloumi in beaten egg white and cook as above. Put ¾ cup pitted black olives, 1 tablespoon drained capers, 1 chopped garlic clove, and 2 tablespoons olive oil into a food processor or blender and whizz for a few seconds until the tapenade is a coarse texture. Spoon onto the golden haloumi, top with a handful of shredded basil leaves, and serve.

black bean soup with soba

Serves **4**
Preparation time **10 minutes**
Cookin g time **8 minutes**

7 oz **dried soba noodles**
2 tablespoons **peanut** or
   vegetable oil
1 bunch of **scallions**, sliced
2 **garlic cloves**, roughly
   chopped
1 **red chili**, seeded and sliced
1½ inch piece of **fresh ginger
   root**, peeled and grated
½ cup **black bean sauce** or
   black bean stir-fry sauce
3 cups **vegetable stock**
2 cups **bok choy** or **collard
   greens**, shredded
2 teaspoons **soy sauce**
1 teaspoon **superfine sugar**
½ cup **raw peanuts**
   (preferably unsalted)

Cook the noodles in a large saucepan of boiling water for 5 minutes or according to the instructions on the package until just tender.

Meanwhile, heat the oil in a saucepan, add the scallions and garlic, and fry gently for 1 minute. Add the chili, ginger, black bean sauce, and stock and bring to a boil. Stir in the bok choy or collard greens, soy sauce, sugar, and peanuts, then reduce the heat and simmer gently for 4 minutes.

Drain the noodles, rinse with fresh hot water, and spoon into 4 warmed soup bowls. Ladle the soup over the top and serve immediately.

For Chinese chicken & black bean soup, cook the noodles as above. Meanwhile, heat the oil in a saucepan, add 3 boneless, skinless chicken thighs, chopped into small chunks, and fry for 4–5 minutes or until cooked through. Add the scallions and garlic and continue as above, replacing the vegetable stock with 3 cups chicken stock and omitting the peanuts.

seared beef & broccoli bruschetta

Serves **4**
Preparation time **5 minutes**
Cooking time **10 minutes**

2¼ cups **broccoli florets**
1 lb **sirloin steak**
⅓ cup **extra virgin olive oil**
4 slices of **sourdough bread**
2 **garlic cloves**, sliced
1 small **red chili**, seeded and
 finely chopped
1 tablespoon **balsamic
 vinegar**
3 cups **baby arugula leaves**
salt and **pepper**

Blanch the broccoli in a saucepan of lightly salted boiling water for 2 minutes. Drain, refresh under cold running water, and drain again. Pat dry on paper towels and set aside.

Rub the steak with 1 tablespoon of the oil and season well with salt and pepper.

Heat a ridged griddle pan over high heat, add the steak, and cook for 2 minutes on each side or until seared all over. The steak should be rare. Remove from the pan and leave to rest for 5 minutes, then cut into thick slices.

While the steak is resting, reheat the griddle pan, add the sourdough bread slices, and cook for 2 minutes on each side or until lightly charred.

Heat the remaining oil in a wok or large skillet, add the garlic and chili, and stir-fry for 1 minute. Add the broccoli and stir-fry for 1 minute. Stir in the vinegar and remove from the heat. Combine with the beef and arugula in a large bowl.

Arrange the bread on serving plates, top with the beef salad, and serve.

For beef bruschetta with horseradish dressing, prepare and cook the steak, and chargrill the sourdough bread as above. Combine the sliced beef with 2 cups watercress leaves in a bowl. Arrange the bread on serving plates and top with the beef and watercress. Beat together 2 tablespoons sour cream, 2 teaspoons horseradish sauce, 1 teaspoon white wine vinegar, and salt and pepper. Drizzle over the bruschetta and serve.

tortilla pizza with salami

Makes **2**
Preparation time **5 minutes**
Cooking time **8–10 minutes**

2 large **flour tortillas** or
  flatbreads
4 tablespoons ready-made
  tomato pasta sauce
3½ oz **spicy salami** slices
5 oz **mozzarella cheese**,
  thinly sliced
1 tablespoon **oregano** leaves,
  plus extra to garnish
salt and **pepper**

Lay the tortillas or flatbreads on 2 large cookie sheets. Top each with half the pasta sauce, spreading it right to the edge. Arrange half the salami and mozzarella slices and oregano leaves on top.

Bake in a preheated oven, 400°F, for 8–10 minutes or until the cheese has melted and is golden. Serve garnished with extra oregano leaves.

For spicy salami, mozzarella & tomato quesadilla, place 1 large flour tortilla or flatbread on the work surface. Top with 2 tablespoons tomato pasta sauce, 2 oz salami slices, ½ cup mozzarella cheese cubes, and a few basil leaves. Add a second tortilla and press flat. Heat a large skillet or ridged griddle pan until hot, add the quesadilla, and cook for 2–3 minutes or until toasted. Flip over and cook on the second side. Cut into wedges to serve.

mustard rarebit

Serves **4**
Preparation time **5 minutes**
Cooking time **10 minutes**

2 tablespoons **butter**
4 **scallions**, thinly sliced
8 oz **Cheddar** or **Red Leicester cheese**, grated
¼ cup **beer**
2 teaspoons **mustard**
4 slices of **wholemeal bread**
pepper

Heat the butter in a skillet, add the scallions, and fry for 5 minutes or until softened.

Reduce the heat to low and stir in the cheese, beer, and mustard. Season well with pepper, then stir slowly for 3–4 minutes or until the cheese has melted.

Meanwhile, toast the bread lightly on both sides and place on a griddle pan. Pour the cheese mixture over the toast and cook under a preheated hot broiler for 1 minute or until bubbling and golden. Serve with a salad of crisp lettuce, radishes, and tomatoes.

For spinach & egg pick-me-ups, lightly toast the bread and set aside. Wilt 4–5 cups spinach leaves in a saucepan with 3 tablespoons water, 1 crushed garlic clove, and some salt and pepper. Drain and squeeze well. Place the wilted spinach on top of the toast and sprinkle with 4 tablespoons grated Parmesan cheese. Poach 4 small eggs in a small saucepan of boiling water (cooking the eggs one at a time and swirling the water well before dropping the eggs in). Cook the toast under a preheated hot broiler until bubbling and golden, then serve the poached eggs on top of the cheese.

pasta,
noodles
& rice

fusilli with parmesan & pine nuts

Serves **4**

Preparation time **5 minutes**

Cooking time **10 minutes**

10 oz fresh or dried **fusilli**

¾ cup **pine nuts**

scant ⅓ cup **butter**

2 tablespoons **olive oil**

handful of **basil leaves**

¾ cup **Parmesan cheese**, grated

salt and **pepper**

Cook the pasta in a large saucepan of salted boiling water or according to the package instructions until al dente.

Meanwhile, toast the pine nuts on a broiler pan under a preheated medium broiler or in a dry skillet over medium heat. Watch them constantly and move them around so they brown evenly. Melt the butter with the oil in a small saucepan.

Drain the pasta and return to the pan. Stir in half the basil leaves so they start to wilt, add the melted butter and oil, season with salt and pepper, and toss well.

Transfer to warmed serving plates, sprinkle with the pine nuts, Parmesan, and the remaining basil leaves, and serve immediately.

For fusilli with red onion & goat cheese, heat the olive oil in a skillet, add 2 finely chopped red onions, and fry gently until softened. Add 2 tablespoons balsamic vinegar and reduce until syrupy. Cook the pasta as above, drain, and stir in the red onion mixture. Spoon into serving bowls, crumble over 7 oz goat cheese and sprinkle with the basil leaves.

bacon & mushroom tagliatelle

Serves **4**
Preparation time **10 minutes**
Cooking time **10 minutes**

12 oz dried **tagliatelle**
1 tablespoon **vegetable oil**
1 **yellow bell pepper**, cored,
    seeded, and chopped
2 **garlic cloves**, crushed
2 cups **mushrooms**, sliced
4 thick slices **bacon,** broiled
    and cut into thin strips
3 tablespoons chopped
    parsley
pepper
2 cups **natural yogurt**
3 tablespoons **pine nuts**,
    toasted (see page 46)

Cook the pasta in a large saucepan of salted boiling water according to the package instructions until al dente.

Meanwhile, heat the oil in a skillet, add the chopped yellow bell pepper, and fry over medium heat for 2–3 minutes. Stir in the garlic, mushrooms, bacon, and parsley, season with pepper, and cook for a further 3 minutes. Reduce the heat to low and stir in the yogurt. Stir and heat through gently.

Drain the pasta and return to the pan. Stir in the sauce, then sprinkle with the pine nuts. Serve immediately with an Italian-style salad and fresh ciabatta bread.

For tagliatelle carbonara, cook the pasta as above. Meanwhile, heat a skillet over medium heat and fry 6 chopped slices of bacon and 3 chopped scallions for 3–4 minutes or until the bacon is crisp and golden. Put 4 egg yolks and ½ cup light cream in a bowl, season with salt and pepper, and whisk well to combine. Drain the pasta and toss through the egg mixture, coating the pasta well, then toss with the bacon mixture and 2 tablespoons chopped parsley. Serve immediately.

noodles with shrimp & bok choy

Serves **4**

Preparation time **5 minutes**

Cooking time **12 minutes**

8 oz dried **medium egg noodles**

3 tablespoons **vegetable oil**

2 tablespoons **sesame seeds**

1 inch piece of **fresh ginger root**, peeled and finely chopped

1 **garlic clove**, crushed

20 raw peeled **jumbo shrimp**

3 tablespoons **light soy sauce**

2 tablespoons **sweet chili sauce**

2 medium-sized heads of **bok choy**, leaves separated

4 **scallions**, finely sliced

handful of **fresh cilantro leaves**, chopped

2 tablespoons **sesame oil**

Cook or soak the noodles according to the package instructions. Drain and set aside.

Heat a large skillet and add 2 tablespoons of the vegetable oil. When really hot, add the noodles, flattening them down so they cover the bottom of the pan. Cook over high heat for 3–4 minutes or until golden brown and crispy. Once they have colored on the first side, turn the noodles over and brown on the other side. Stir in the sesame seeds.

Meanwhile, heat the remaining oil in a wok or large skillet, add the ginger and garlic, and stir-fry for 1 minute. Then add the shrimp and stir-fry for 2 minutes or until turning pink. Add the soy sauce and sweet chili sauce and bring to a boil, then reduce the heat and simmer for 1–2 minutes or until the shrimp are pink and firm. Finally, add the bok choy and stir until the leaves begin to wilt.

Place the noodles on a large plate and top with the shrimp and bok choy. Sprinkle with the scallions and cilantro and drizzle with the sesame oil.

For shrimp & lemongrass stir-fry, heat a little vegetable oil in a wok, add 2 finely chopped shallots, 2 finely chopped lemongrass stalks, 1 seeded and finely chopped red chilli, 1 crushed garlic clove, and a ¾ inch piece of fresh ginger root, peeled and finely chopped, and stir-fry for 2 minutes. Add 20 raw peeled jumbo shrimp and stir-fry until pink. Add 6 tablespoons light soy sauce, 2 tablespoons sesame oil, and the juice of 1 lime. Finally, add 2 tablespoons roughly chopped fresh cilantro and serve.

fried rice with beans & tofu

Serves **4**
Preparation time **10 minutes**
Cooking time **10 minutes**

about 1 ½ pints **sunflower oil**,
   for deep-frying
8 oz block ready-fried **tofu**,
   cubed
2 **eggs**
1 cup cold cooked **rice**
1 ½–2 tablespoons **light soy
   sauce**
2 teaspoons crushed dried
   chilies
1 teaspoon **fish sauce** or **salt**
1 cup **green beans**, trimmed
   and finely chopped
mint leaves, to garnish

Heat the oil in a deep heatproof saucepan and deep-fry the tofu over medium heat until golden brown on all sides. Remove from the oil with a slotted spoon, drain on paper towels, and set aside.

Spoon 2 tablespoonfuls of the hot oil into a wok. Keeping the oil hot, break the eggs into it, breaking up the yolks and stirring them around.

Add the rice, 1 ½ tablespoons of the soy sauce, chilies, fish sauce or salt, and green beans, and stir-fry for 3–4 minutes. Stir in the tofu and warm through with the rice for another 2–3 minutes. Add the remaining soy sauce to taste if liked.

Transfer to a serving dish and serve immediately with mint leaves scattered on top.

For quick shrimp-fried rice, heat 2 tablespoons peanut oil in a wok or large skillet over very high heat, add 1 cup cold cooked rice, 1 tablespoon peeled and grated fresh ginger root, 3 small seeded and chopped red chilies, 4 sliced scallions, and 1 lb small raw peeled shrimp. Cook for 5 minutes or until the shrimp turn pink and are cooked through. Sprinkle with 2 tablespoons soy sauce and serve.

pesto alla genovese

Serves **4**
Preparation time **10 minutes**
Cooking time **15 minutes**

3 cups **basil leaves**
3 tablespoons **pine nuts**
2 **garlic cloves**, crushed
2 tablespoons grated
   Parmesan, plus extra to
   serve
1 tablespoon grated **pecorino
   cheese**
3 tablespoons **olive oil**
8 oz **baby new potatoes**,
   scrubbed and thinly sliced
13 oz dried **trenette** or
   linguine
1 cup **fine green beans**,
   trimmed

Grind the basil, pine nuts, and garlic using a large mortar and pestle until the mixture forms a paste. Stir in the cheeses, then slowly add the oil, a little at a time, stirring continuously with a wooden spoon. Alternatively, blend the basil, pine nuts, and garlic in a food processor until the mixture forms a paste. Add the cheeses and process briefly, then, with the motor still running, pour in the oil through the feed tube in a thin, steady stream.

Cook the potatoes in a large saucepan of salted boiling water for 5 minutes, then add the pasta and cook according to the package instructions until al dente. Add the beans 5 minutes before the end of the cooking time.

Drain the pasta and vegetables, reserving 2 tablespoons of the cooking water. Return the cooked pasta and vegetables to the pan and stir in the pesto sauce, adding the reserved water to loosen the mixture. Serve immediately, with some extra grated Parmesan.

For pesto penne with sun-dried tomatoes & feta, make the pesto as above. Cook 13 oz penne in a large saucepan of salted boiling water according to the package instructions until al dente. Meanwhile, toast a handful of pine nuts in a skillet until golden, being careful not to let them burn, and chop 8 sun-dried tomatoes and set aside. Drain the pasta, stir through the pesto and sun-dried tomatoes, and sprinkle with the pine nuts and ⅔ cup crumbled feta cheese. Serve immediately with a green salad.

prosciutto & porcini pappardelle

Serves 4
Preparation time **10 minutes**
Cooking time about **10 minutes**

13 oz fresh or dried **pappardelle**
2 tablespoons **olive oil**
1 **garlic clove**, crushed
8 oz fresh **porcini mushrooms**, sliced
8 oz **prosciutto** slices
⅔ cup **whipping cream**
handful of **parsley**, chopped
3 oz **Parmesan cheese**, grated
salt and **pepper**

Cook the pasta in a large saucepan of salted boiling water according to the package instructions until al dente.

Meanwhile, heat the oil in a large saucepan over medium heat, add the garlic and porcini, and sauté for 4 minutes. Cut the prosciutto into strips, keeping them separate. Add to the porcini mixture with the cream and parsley, and season with salt and pepper. Bring to a boil, then reduce the heat and simmer for 1 minute.

Drain the pasta, add to the sauce, and toss well. Scatter with the Parmesan, toss well, and serve immediately.

For spaghetti with dried porcini & pine nuts, soak 4 oz dried porcini in enough hot water to cover for 15 minutes to rehydrate them. Drain, reserving the water, and pat dry with paper towels. Cook 13 oz dried spaghetti as above. Meanwhile, fry the porcini as above, then add the reserved soaking water to the pan, and boil until the liquid has almost evaporated. Stir in the prosciutto and cream as above. Briefly toast 2 tablespoons pine nuts in a skillet and add to the sauce. Drain the pasta, add to the sauce, and toss well. Serve immediately.

tuna-layered lasagne with arugula

Serves **4**
Preparation time **10 minutes**
Cooking time **10 minutes**

8 dried **lasagne** sheets
1 tablespoon **olive oil**
1 bunch of **scallions**, sliced
2 **zucchini**, diced
1 lb **cherry tomatoes**,
  quartered
2 x 7 oz cans **tuna** in water,
  drained
3 cups **wild arugula**
4 teaspoons **pesto**
pepper
basil leaves, to garnish

Cook the pasta sheets, in batches, in a large saucepan of salted boiling water according to the package instructions until al dente. Drain and return to the pan to keep warm.

Meanwhile, heat the oil in a skillet over medium heat, add the scallions and zucchini, and sauté for 3 minutes. Remove the pan from the heat, add the tomatoes, tuna, and arugula and gently toss everything together.

Place a little of the tuna mixture on 4 serving plates and top each with a pasta sheet. Spoon over the remaining tuna mixture, then top with the remaining pasta sheets. Season with plenty of pepper and top each with a spoonful of pesto and some basil leaves before serving.

For salmon lasagne, use 14 oz fresh salmon. Pan-fry the for 2–3 minutes on each side or until cooked through, remove the bones and skin, then flake and use in place of the tuna.

veggie carbonara

Serves **4**
Preparation time **5 minutes**
Cooking time **15 minutes**

13 oz dried **penne**
2 tablespoons **olive oil**
2 **garlic cloves,** finely chopped
3 **zucchini,** thinly sliced
6 **scallions,** cut into ½ inch
  pieces
4 **egg yolks**
½ cup **crème fraîche**
3 oz **Parmesan cheese,**
  grated, plus extra to serve
salt and **pepper**

Cook the pasta in a large saucepan of salted boiling water according to the package instructions until al dente.

Heat the oil in a heavy-based skillet over medium-high heat, add the garlic, zucchini, and scallions, and sauté for 4–5 minutes or until the zucchini is tender. Remove the pan from the heat and set aside.

Meanwhile, put the egg yolks in a bowl and season with salt and a generous grinding of pepper. Mix together with a fork.

Just before the pasta is ready, return the pan with the zucchini mixture to the heat. Stir in the crème fraîche and bring to a boil.

Drain the pasta well, return to the pan, and immediately stir in the egg mixture, Parmesan, and the creamy zucchini mixture. Combine well and serve immediately with a scattering of extra grated Parmesan.

For asparagus carbonara, replace the zucchini with 8 oz asparagus spears. Cut the spears into 1 inch pieces and cook in the same way as the zucchini.

thai chicken noodle salad

Serves **4**
Preparation time **10 minutes**
Cooking time **10 minutes**

8 oz dried **thin rice noodles**
6 tablespoons **Thai sweet chili sauce**
2 tablespoons **Thai fish sauce**
juice of 2 **limes**
2 cooked boneless, skinless **chicken breasts**
1 **cucumber**, cut into ribbons
1 **red chili**, seeded and finely chopped
small handful of **fresh cilantro leaves**

Put the noodles in a large heatproof bowl, pour over boiling water to cover, and leave to stand for 6–8 minutes, or according to the package instructions, until tender. Drain and rinse under cold running water.

Whisk together the sweet chili sauce, fish sauce, and lime juice in a large bowl. Shred the chicken breasts and toss with the dressing to coat.

Add the noodles, cucumber, and chilli to the chicken mixture and toss gently to combine. Scatter over the cilantro leaves and serve immediately.

For seafood noodle salad, cook the noodles as above. Prepare the dressing but replace the chicken with 1 lb cooked peeled shrimp and 7 oz cooked shelled mussels. Scatter over a small handful of basil leaves instead of cilantro leaves.

creamy blue cheese pasta

Serves **4**
Preparation time **10 minutes**
Cooking time **10 minutes**

12 oz dried **pasta shells**
2 tablespoons **olive oil**
6 **scallions**, thinly sliced
5 oz **dolcelatte cheese**, diced
1 scant cup **cream cheese**
salt and **pepper**
3 tablespoons chopped
   chives, to garnish

Cook the pasta in a large saucepan of salted boiling water according to the package instructions until al dente.

Meanwhile, heat the olive oil in a large skillet, add the scallions, and cook over medium heat for 2–3 minutes. Add the cheeses and stir to blend into a smooth sauce.

Drain the pasta and transfer to a warmed serving bowl. Stir in the sauce and season to taste with salt and pepper. Sprinkle with the chives and serve immediately.

For cheese & leek filo parcels, fry 3 thinly sliced leeks in the oil until softened and beginning to brown, then leave to cool. Mix with the cheeses as above and 3 tablespoons chopped chives. Melt 1 heaping ¼ cup butter in a saucepan. Put 8 sheets of filo pastry on a plate and cover with a damp tea towel. Working with a single sheet of pastry at a time, cut into 3 equal strips and brush well with melted butter. Put a teaspoon of the cheese mixture at one end of each strip. Fold one corner diagonally over to enclose and continue folding to the end of the strip to make a triangular parcel. Brush with melted butter and place on a cookie sheet. Repeat with the remaining cheese mixture and pastry to make about 24 small parcels. Bake in a preheated oven, 425°F, for 8–10 minutes or until golden brown. Serve hot.

tagliatelle with crab sauce

Serves **4**
Preparation time **5 minutes**
Cooking time **15 minutes**

10 oz fresh or dried **tagliatelle**
2 tablespoons **olive oil**
2 **shallots**, chopped
7 oz fresh **crab meat**
1–2 pinches of crushed dried
   chilies
grated zest and juice of
   1 **lemon**
¾ cup **heavy cream**
handful of **chives**, snipped
salt and **pepper**
3 oz **Parmesan cheese**,
   grated, to serve

Cook the pasta in a large saucepan of boiling water or according to the package instructions until al dente.

Heat the oil in a saucepan, add the shallots, and fry gently until softened but not browned. Add the crab meat, chilies, lemon zest and juice, and salt and pepper to taste.

Add the cream to the crab mixture and bring to a boil, then stir in the chives.

Drain the pasta well and return to the pan. Stir in the crab sauce, toss well, and serve immediately with a bowl of grated Parmesan.

For creamy tagliatelle with imitation crab legs & dill sauce, cook the pasta as above. Meanwhile, add 2 large crushed garlic cloves with the shallots and fry as above. Add ¼ pint white wine, 4 tablespoons heavy cream, and a handful of fresh chopped dill. Finally, mix the drained pasta and 8oz shredded imitation crab legs into the creamy sauce, season with salt and pepper, and serve. (Imitation crab legs are also known as "Krab.")

tuna, spinach & tomato penne

Serves **4**
Preparation time **5 minutes**
Cooking time **10 minutes**

11½ oz dried **penne**
2 tablespoons **olive oil**, plus
    extra for drizzling
1 **onion,** finely sliced
1 **garlic clove,** crushed
1 lb **cherry tomatoes,** halved
pinch of **sugar** (optional)
8 oz **baby leaf spinach**
2 x 6½ oz cans **tuna steak** in
    olive oil, drained
salt and **pepper**

Cook the pasta in a large saucepan of salted boiling water according to the package instructions until al dente.

Meanwhile, heat the oil in a large saucepan, add the onion, and fry gently until softened. Add the garlic and tomatoes and fry for a further 3–4 minutes or until the tomatoes just begin to break up. Season with salt and pepper and a little sugar if needed.

Stir in the spinach, then gently stir in the tuna, trying not to break it up too much.

Drain the pasta, add to the sauce, and toss well. Drizzle a little more olive oil over the pasta before serving.

For creamy penne pasta with mussels & white wine, cook the penne as above. Meanwhile, heat a little oil in a saucepan and add 1 finely chopped garlic clove, ½ cup white wine and 3 lb scrubbed and debearded mussels to the pan (first discarding any that don't shut when tapped). Cover and cook until the mussels have opened. Discard any that remain closed. Strain the mussels through a sieve, reserving the liquid. Pour the liquid back into a clean saucepan and add a scant cup of heavy cream. Simmer until it reaches a creamy consistency. Drain the pasta. Pick the mussels from their shells and add to the sauce along with the pasta. Season with salt and pepper.

linguine with ham & eggs

Serves **2**
Preparation time **5 minutes**
Cooking time **10 minutes**

5 oz dried **linguine**
2 **eggs**
3 oz thinly sliced **ham**
2 **scallions**, thinly sliced

Mustard dressing
3 tablespoons chopped
   parsley
1 tablespoon **wholegrain
   mustard**
2 teaspoons **lemon juice**
good pinch of **superfine
   sugar**
3 tablespoons **olive oil**
salt and **pepper**

Cook the pasta in a saucepan of salted boiling water according to the package instructions until al dente.

Meanwhile, put the eggs in a small saucepan and just cover with cold water. Bring to a boil, then reduce to a gentle simmer and cook for 4 minutes (once the water boils the eggs will usually start to move around).

Roll up the ham and slice it as thinly as possible. Meanwhile, make the mustard dressing. Mix together the parsley, mustard, lemon juice, sugar, oil, and a little salt and pepper in a bowl.

Drain the eggs, rinse in cold water, then crack the shells and peel once cool enough to handle.

Add the scallions to the pan of pasta 30 seconds before the end of the cooking time, then drain and return to the pan. Stir in the ham and the mustard dressing and pile onto warm serving plates. Halve the peeled eggs and serve on top.

For linguine with lemon cream, cook the pasta as above, adding 14½ oz trimmed asparagus to the pan 3 minutes before the end of the cooking time. Meanwhile, put the grated zest of ½ lemon, 1¼ cups chicken stock, and 1¼ cups crème fraîche into a saucepan and heat through gently. Add the juice of 1 lemon and ¾ cup grated Parmesan cheese and cook until the sauce has thickened. Drain the pasta and asparagus, stir in the lemon cream and some chopped parsley, and season with pepper. Serve immediately.

rice noodles with lemon chicken

Serves **4**

Preparation time **10 minutes**

Cooking time **10 minutes**

4 boneless **chicken breasts**,
  skin on, each 5 oz

juice of 2 **lemons**

4 tablespoons **sweet chili
  sauce**

8 oz dried **rice noodles**

small bunch of **parsley**,
  chopped

small bunch of **cilantro**,
  chopped

½ **cucumber**, peeled into
  ribbons with a vegetable
  peeler

salt and **pepper**

finely chopped **red chili**, to
  garnish

Lay a chicken breast between 2 sheets of plastic wrap and flatten with a rolling pin. Repeat with the remaining chicken breasts.

Mix the chicken with half the lemon juice and the sweet chili sauce in a large nonmetallic dish and season to taste with salt and pepper.

Arrange the chicken breasts on a broiler rack in a single layer. Cook under a preheated hot broiler for 4–5 minutes on each side or until cooked through. Finish on the skin side so that it is crisp.

Meanwhile, put the noodles in a large heatproof bowl, pour over boiling water to cover, and leave for 10 minutes or according to the package instructions, until tender, then drain. Return to the bowl, add the remaining lemon juice, herbs, and cucumber to the noodles and toss well to mix. Season to taste with salt and pepper.

Top the noodles with the cooked chicken and serve immediately, garnished with the chopped red chili.

For stir-fried ginger broccoli, to serve as a side dish, trim 1 lb broccoli. Divide the heads into florets, then diagonally slice the stalks. Blanch the florets and stalks in a saucepan of salted boiling water for 30 seconds. Drain, refresh under cold running water, and drain again thoroughly. Heat 2 tablespoons vegetable oil in a large skillet, add 1 thinly sliced garlic clove and a 1 inch piece of fresh ginger root, peeled and finely chopped, and stir-fry for a few seconds. Add the broccoli and stir-fry for 2 minutes. Add 1 teaspoon sesame oil and fry for a further 30 seconds.

speck, spinach & taleggio fusilli

Serves **4**
Preparation time **5 minutes**
Cooking time **15 minutes**

12 oz dried **fusilli**
3½ oz **speck** slices
5 oz **Taleggio cheese**, rind removed and discarded, the cheese cut into small cubes
½ cup **heavy cream**
4 cups **baby leaf spinach**, roughly chopped
salt and **pepper**
grated **Parmesan cheese**, to serve (optional)

Cook the pasta in a large saucepan of salted boiling water according to the package instructions until al dente.

Meanwhile, cut the speck into wide strips.

Drain the pasta, return it to the pan, and place over low heat. Add the speck, Taleggio, cream, and spinach and stir until most of the cheese has melted. Season with a generous grinding of pepper and serve immediately with a scattering of grated Parmesan, if liked.

For mozzarella & ham fusilli, use 5 oz mozzarella instead of the Taleggio and replace the speck with 3½ oz Black Forest ham. Mozzarella will give a milder flavor than Taleggio.

chinese stir-fry noodles

Serves **4**

Preparation time **10 minutes**

Cooking time **10 minutes**

1 cup **frozen peas**

6 oz dried **egg noodles**

2 tablespoons **vegetable oil**

1 bunch of **scallions**, sliced

10 oz pack mixed **stir-fry vegetables** (shredded cabbage, baby corn, bean sprouts, bell peppers etc.)

10 oz **firm tofu**, cubed

½ cup **hoisin sauce**

3 tablespoons **orange juice**

salt and **pepper**

Cook the peas in a saucepan of boiling water for 2 minutes. Drain well. Cook or soak the noodles according to the package instructions.

Meanwhile, heat the oil in a wok or large skillet. Add the scallions and ready-prepared vegetables and stir-fry for 3–4 minutes or until softened. Add the tofu, peas, hoisin sauce, and orange juice and stir for 1 minute.

Drain the noodles, add to the pan, toss everything together, and season to taste with salt and pepper. Serve immediately.

For Chinese lamb & broccoli stir-fry, replace the tofu with 13 oz lamb leg steak, fat removed and cut into strips 1 x ¼ inch in size, and stir-fry for 2 minutes. Cut 7 oz broccoli into florets and blanch for 2 minutes. Drain and add to the stir-fried vegetables. Mix with the hoisin sauce and noodles as above, omitting the orange juice.

one pot

15-minute soup

Serves **4–6**
Preparation time **10 minutes**
Cooking time about **15 minutes**

2 tablespoons **olive oil**
1 small **onion**, finely chopped
2 **garlic cloves**, finely chopped
2 thick slices of day-old **bread**, crusts removed, broken into pieces
2 **tomatoes**, roughly chopped
4¼ cups **vegetable stock**
1⅓ cups frozen **peas**
1 teaspoon **pimentón dulce** (mild paprika)
½ cup **fino sherry**
8 oz raw **jumbo shrimp**, peeled
1 **hard-boiled egg**, peeled and finely chopped
2 tablespoons finely chopped **parsley**
salt and **pepper**

Heat the oil in a saucepan, add the onion, garlic, and bread and cook over medium heat, stirring frequently, for 3–4 minutes.

Stir in the tomatoes, stock, peas, pimentón, and sherry and bring to a boil. Reduce the heat and cook over medium heat, stirring occasionally, for 3–4 minutes.

Add the shrimp and cook, stirring, for 5–7 minutes or until the shrimp turn pink and are cooked through. Remove the pan from the heat and season to taste with salt and pepper.

Ladle into warmed shallow bowls, scatter over the egg and parsley, and serve immediately.

For Indian chicken & chickpea soup, pour a 13 oz can chopped tomatoes and 1¾ cups water in a saucepan, stir together, and warm through over low heat. Meanwhile, chop 4 cooked chicken breasts into chunky pieces, removing any skin, and shred 5 oz Savoy cabbage. Stir the chicken, cabbage, 2 teaspoons curry paste, a drained 13 oz can chickpeas, and 1 crumbled chicken or vegetable stock cube into the tomatoes. Stir well, cover, and cook over high heat for 6 minutes or until the soup is piping hot and the cabbage is just tender. Serve with warm garlic naan bread.

green bean, miso & noodle soup

Serves **2**
Preparation time **10 minutes**
Cooking time **10 minutes**

3 tablespoons **brown miso
    paste**
4¼ cups **vegetable stock**
1 oz **fresh ginger root,** peeled
    and grated
2 **garlic cloves**, thinly sliced
1 small **hot red chili**, seeded
    and thinly sliced
3½ oz **dried soba,
    wholemeal,** or **plain
    noodles**
1 bunch of **scallions**, finely
    shredded
⅔ cup fresh or frozen **peas**
1⅔ cups **green beans**,
    trimmed and shredded
3 tablespoons **mirin**
1 tablespoon **sugar**
1 tablespoon **rice wine
    vinegar**

Blend the miso paste with a little of the stock in a
saucepan to make a thick, smooth paste. Add a little
more stock to thin the paste and then pour in the
remainder. Add the ginger, garlic, and chili and bring
almost to a boil.

Reduce the heat to a gentle simmer, add the noodles,
stirring until they have softened into the stock, and cook
for about 5 minutes or until the noodles are just tender.

Add the scallions, peas, green beans, mirin, sugar, and
vinegar and stir well.

Cook gently for 1–2 minutes or until the vegetables
have softened. Ladle into bowls and serve immediately.

For miso soup with tofu, make dashi stock by boiling
½ oz kombu seaweed in 3 pints of water in a very large
saucepan, skimming off any scum that rises to the
surface. Add 1½ tablespoons dried bonito flakes and
simmer, uncovered, for 15 minutes. Strain the stock and
return to the pan with 2 tablespoons red or white miso,
stirring until dissolved. Cut 1 small leek into fine julienne
strips and 4 oz firm tofu into small squares and add to
the warm soup with 1 tablespoon wakame seaweed.
Garnish with chopped chives.

mushrooms à la greque

Serves **4**
Preparation time **10 minutes**,
   plus standing
Cooking time **10 minutes**

½ cup **olive oil**
2 large **onions**, sliced
3 **garlic cloves**, finely chopped
1 ¼ lb **button mushrooms**,
   halved
8 **plum tomatoes**, roughly
   chopped or 13 oz can
   chopped tomatoes
¾ cup **pitted black olives**
2 tablespoons **white wine**
   vinegar
salt and **pepper**
chopped **parsley**, to garnish

Heat 2 tablespoons of the oil in a large pan, add the
onions and garlic, and fry until softened and beginning
to brown. Add the mushrooms and tomatoes and cook,
stirring gently, for 4–5 minutes, then add the olives.

Whisk the remaining oil with the vinegar in a small
bowl, season to taste with salt and pepper, and drizzle
over the salad.

Garnish with the chopped parsley, cover, and leave to
stand at room temperature for 30 minutes to allow the
flavors to mingle before serving.

For mushroom pasta salad, prepare the mushroom
mixture as above. Cook 7 oz dried pennette or farfalle
in a large saucepan of salted boiling water according
to the package instructions until al dente. Meanwhile,
cook 1 ¼ cups trimmed green beans in a saucepan of
salted boiling water until just tender. Drain the beans,
refresh under cold running water, and drain again. Drain
the pasta well and toss into the mushroom mixture with
the beans and 2 tablespoons torn basil leaves. Serve at
room temperature.

spicy fried rice with spinach

Serves **3–4**
Preparation time **10 minutes**
Cooking time **10 minutes**

4 eggs
2 tablespoons **sherry**
2 tablespoons **light soy sauce**
1 bunch of **scallions**
4 tablespoons **peanut oil**
½ cup **unsalted cashews**
1 **green bell pepper**, seeded
  and finely chopped
½ teaspoon **Chinese five-
  spice powder**
1⅓ cups ready-cooked **long-
  grain rice**
5 cups **baby leaf spinach**
3½ oz **sprouted mung beans**
  or 2 oz **pea shoots**
salt and **pepper**

Beat the eggs with the sherry and 1 tablespoon of the soy sauce in a small bowl. Cut 2 of the scallions into 3 inch lengths, then cut these lengthways into fine shreds. Leave in a bowl of very cold water to curl up slightly. Finely chop the remaining scallions, keeping the white and green parts separate.

Heat half the oil in a wok or large skillet, add the cashews and green parts of the scallions and fry, turning in the oil, until the cashews are lightly browned. Remove with a slotted spoon and drain on paper towels.

Add the white parts of the scallions to the pan and stir-fry for 1 minute. Add the beaten eggs and cook, stirring continuously, until the egg begins to scramble into small pieces rather than one omelette.

Stir in the green bell pepper and five-spice powder with the remaining oil and cook for 1 minute, then tip in the cooked rice and spinach with the remaining soy sauce, mixing the ingredients together well until thoroughly combined and the spinach has wilted.

Return the cashews and scallions to the pan with the mung beans or pea shoots and season to taste with salt and pepper. Pile onto serving plates, scatter with the drained scallion curls, and serve with sweet chili sauce.

For spicy fried rice with baby corn, replace the spinach with ½ small shredded Chinese cabbage and 2 cups sliced baby corn and add to the pan with the green bell pepper.

chickpeas with chorizo

Serves **4**
Preparation time **10 minutes**
Cooking time about **10
 minutes**

2 tablespoons **olive oil**
1 **red onion**, finely chopped
2 **garlic cloves**, crushed
7 oz **chorizo sausage**, cut into
 ½ inch dice
2 **ripe tomatoes**, seeded and
 finely chopped
3 tablespoons chopped
 parsley
2 x 13 oz cans **chickpeas**,
 drained
salt and **pepper**

Heat the oil in a large nonstick skillet, add the onion, garlic, and chorizo and cook over medium-high heat, stirring frequently, for 4–5 minutes.

Add the tomatoes, parsley, and chickpeas to the skillet and cook, stirring frequently, for 4–5 minutes or until heated through.

Season to taste with salt and pepper and serve immediately or leave to cool to room temperature. Serve with crusty bread.

For harissa-spiced chickpeas with haloumi & spinach, heat the oil in a large saucepan, add 2 chopped onions and the garlic, omitting the chorizo, and cook over low heat until softened. Omit the fresh tomatoes and parsley and add 2 tablespoons harissa paste, the chickpeas and 2 x 13 oz cans chopped tomatoes to the pan. Bring to a boil, then reduce the heat and simmer for about 5 minutes. Add 8 oz cubed haloumi cheese and 6 cups baby leaf spinach and cook over low heat for a further 5 minutes. Season to taste with salt and pepper and stir in the juice of 1 lemon. Serve with grated Parmesan cheese and warm crusty bread.

tomato rice

Serves **4**

Preparation time **5 minutes,**
plus soaking and standing

Cooking time **15 minutes**

1¼ cups **basmati rice**

2 tablespoons **butter**

1 small **onion**, halved and
thinly sliced

1 **garlic clove**, crushed

1 teaspoon **cumin seeds**

4–6 black **peppercorns**

1 **clove**

1 **cinnamon stick**

⅓ cup **frozen peas**

7 oz can **chopped tomatoes**

2 tablespoons **tomato paste**

2 cups **boiling water**

2 tablespoons chopped **fresh
cilantro**

salt and **pepper**

Rinse the basmati rice under cold running water, put it in a bowl, and cover with cold water. Soak for 15 minutes, then drain well.

Heat the butter in a large heavy-based saucepan, add the onion, garlic, cumin, peppercorns, clove, and cinnamon and stir-fry for 2–3 minutes. Add the peas, tomatoes, tomato paste, and drained rice and stir-fry for another 2–3 minutes.

Add the boiling water and cilantro, season with salt and pepper, and bring back to a boil. Cover tightly, reduce the heat to low, and simmer gently for 10 minutes. Do not lift the lid because the steam is required for the cooking process.

Remove the pan from the heat and leave the rice to stand, covered and undisturbed, for 8–10 minutes. To serve, fluff up the grains of rice with a fork.

For quick paella-style rice, soak the rice as above. Stir-fry the onion and garlic as above, omitting the cumin, clove, and cinnamon. Add 1 cored, seeded, and chopped yellow bell pepper and 5 oz diced chorizo with the peas, tomatoes, and rice, omitting the tomato paste, and stir-fry as above. Add the boiling water, 1 teaspoon saffron threads, and 1 teaspoon paprika. Season with salt and pepper, and cook as above. Midway through the steaming process, add 7 oz cooked frozen large shrimp, then continue cooking with the lid on for 3 minutes until the shrimp are piping hot. Serve as above.

spinach & gorgonzola gnocchi

Serves **3–4**
Preparation time **5 minutes**
Cooking time **10 minutes**

1 ¼ cups **vegetable stock**
1 lb **potato gnocchi**
5 oz **Gorgonzola cheese**, cut
   into small pieces
3 tablespoons **heavy cream**
plenty of freshly grated
   nutmeg
8 cups **baby leaf spinach**
pepper

Bring the stock to a boil in a large saucepan. Tip in the gnocchi and return to a boil. Cook for 2–3 minutes or until plumped up and tender.

Stir in the cheese, cream, and nutmeg and heat until the cheese melts to make a creamy sauce.

Add the spinach to the pan and cook gently for 1–2 minutes, turning the spinach with the gnocchi and sauce until wilted. Pile onto serving plates and season with plenty of pepper.

For sage & Parmesan gnocchi, cook the gnocchi in the vegetable stock as above. Meanwhile, heat ⅓ cup butter in a skillet, add 2 crushed garlic cloves, and fry over low heat for 1 minute or until the garlic turns golden brown. Add 16 sage leaves and allow the butter to froth while the sage crisps. Drain the gnocchi, return to the skillet, and stir in the sage butter. Serve with grated Parmesan and a mixed green salad.

thai chicken curry

Serves **4**
Preparation time **5 minutes**
Cooking time **15 minutes**

1 tablespoon **sunflower oil**
1 tablespoon **Thai green curry paste** (see below)
6 **kaffir lime leaves**, torn
2 tablespoons **Thai fish sauce**
1 tablespoon **soft light brown sugar**
¾ cup **chicken stock**
14 fl oz can **coconut milk**
1 lb boneless, skinless **chicken thigh fillets**, diced
4 oz can **bamboo shoots**, drained
4 oz can **baby corn**, drained
large handful of **Thai basil leaves** or **fresh cilantro leaves**, plus extra to garnish
1 tablespoon **lime juice**
1 **red chili**, seeded and sliced, to garnish

Heat the oil in a wok or large skillet, add the curry paste and lime leaves, and stir-fry over low heat for 1–2 minutes or until fragrant.

Stir in the fish sauce, sugar, stock, and coconut milk and bring to a boil, then reduce the heat and simmer gently for 5 minutes.

Add the chicken and cook for 5 minutes. Add the bamboo shoots and baby corn and cook for a further 3 minutes or until the chicken is cooked through.

Stir through the basil or cilantro leaves and lime juice, then serve garnished with the extra leaves and chili.

For homemade Thai green curry paste, put 15 small green chilies, 4 halved garlic cloves, 2 finely chopped lemongrass stalks, 2 torn Kaffir lime leaves, 2 chopped shallots, 1 inch piece of fresh ginger root, peeled and finely chopped, 2 teaspoons black peppercorns, 1 teaspoon pared lime zest, ½ teaspoon salt, and 1 tablespoon peanut oil in a food processor or blender and blend to a thick paste. Transfer to a screw-top jar. This makes a generous ½ cup of paste, which can be stored in the refrigerator for up to 3 weeks.

cambodian fish hotpot

Serves **4**
Preparation time **10 minutes**
Cooking time **15 minutes**

1 teaspoon **sesame oil**
1 tablespoon **vegetable oil**
3 **shallots**, chopped
3 **garlic cloves**, crushed
1 **onion**, halved and sliced
20 fl oz **coconut milk**
3 tablespoons **rice wine vinegar**
1 **lemongrass stalk**, chopped
4 **kaffir lime** leaves
3–6 **red bird's eye chilies**, halved and seeds removed
1 1/4 cups **fish stock**
1 tablespoon **superfine sugar**
2 **tomatoes**, quartered
2 tablespoons **fish sauce**
1 teaspoon **tomato paste**
6 oz **live clams**, cleaned,
12 oz raw peeled **jumbo shrimp**
4 oz **squid**, cleaned and cut into rings
13 oz can **straw mushrooms**, drained
20 **holy basil leaves**, optional

Heat the sesame and vegetable oils together in a large dutch oven, add the shallots and garlic, and fry gently for 2 minutes or until softened but not browned.

Add the onion, coconut water, rice wine vinegar, lemongrass, lime leaves, chilies, stock, and sugar to the pot and bring to a boil. Boil for 2 minutes, then reduce the heat and add the tomatoes, fish sauce, and tomato paste, and cook for 5 minutes.

Discard any clams that don't shut when tapped, then add them with the shrimp, squid rings, and mushrooms to the pot and simmer gently for 5–6 minutes or until the shrimp turn pink, the squid are cooked through, and the clams have opened. Discard any clams that remain closed. Stir in the basil leaves if liked.

Serve the hotpot immediately with rice noodles.

For traditional fisherman's stew, replace the sesame and vegetable oils with olive oil and fry the garlic and shallots as above. When adding the onion, replace the coconut milk, rice wine vinegar, lemongrass, lime leaves, chilies, stock, and sugar with 2 x 13 oz cans chopped tomatoes, 1 pinch saffron threads, 1 1/4 cups white wine and 1 1/4 lb white fish fillets, skinned and cut into bite-sized chunks. Continue as above, adding the tomatoes, fish sauce, and tomato paste, then the shrimp, squid rings, and mushrooms, but replace the basil leaves with chopped parsley. Serve with crusty bread instead of the noodles, dipping sauce, and fresh cilantro.

thai monkfish & shrimp curry

Serves **4**
Preparation time **10 minutes**
Cooking time **8 minutes**

3 tablespoons **Thai green curry paste**
14 fl oz can **coconut milk**
1 **lemongrass stalk** (optional), halved lengthwise
2 **kaffir lime leaves** (fresh or dried, optional)
1 tablespoon **soft brown sugar**
10 oz **monkfish or cod loins,** cubed
½ cup **green beans**, trimmed
12 raw peeled **jumbo shrimp**
2–3 tablespoons **Thai fish sauce**
2 tablespoons fresh **lime juice**

To garnish
fresh cilantro sprigs
sliced **green chilies**

Put the curry paste and coconut milk in a saucepan. Bruise the lemongrass stalk, by bashing with a rolling pin, and add it to the pan with lime leaves, if using, and sugar. Bring to a boil, then add the monkfish. Simmer gently for 2 minutes, then add the beans and cook for a further 2 minutes or until the fish is cooked through.

Stir in the shrimp, fish sauce, and lime juice and cook for 2–5 minutes until the shrimp turn pink and are cooked through.

Transfer the curry to a warm serving dish and top with cilantro sprigs and chili slices. Serve with plain boiled rice.

For Malaysian monkfish & shrimp curry, heat 2 tablespoons sunflower oil in a saucepan, add 2 thinly sliced onions and fry gently until softened. Replace the curry paste with 2 tablespoons lemongrass paste, 1 tablespoon garlic paste, 1 seeded and diced red chili, 1¾ inch piece of fresh ginger root, peeled and grated, 1 teaspoon turmeric, 1 cinnamon stick, and 2 star anise and add to the onions with the coconut milk, lemongrass, and lime leaves, if using, sugar, and salt. Continue as above.

meaty treats

spicy pork patties

Makes **12**
Preparation time **10 minutes**,
    plus chilling
Cooking time **6–8 minutes**

14½ oz **ground pork**
3 teaspoons **hot curry paste**
3 tablespoons fresh
    breadcrumbs
1 small **onion**, finely chopped
2 tablespoons **lime juice**
2 tablespoons chopped
    cilantro
1 **red chili**, seeded and finely
    chopped
2 teaspoons **soft brown
    sugar**
sunflower oil, for frying
salt and **pepper**

To serve
⅔ cup **plain yogurt**
3 tablspoons chopped **fresh
    cilantro**

Put the pork, curry paste, breadcrumbs, onion, lime juice, cilantro, chili, and sugar into a large bowl and, using your hands, mix until thoroughly blended. Season with salt and pepper, cover, and chill for 30 minutes or until ready to cook.

Divide the mixture into 12 portions and shape each one into a flat, round patty.

Heat the oil in a large nonstick skillet and cook the patties over medium heat for 3–4 minutes on each side or until cooked through. Remove with a slotted spoon and drain on paper towels. Mix the yogurt with the chopped cilantro and serve in a small dish alongside the patties, with rice and a salad.

For herby lamb patties, put 1 lb lean ground lamb, 3 tablespoons fresh breadcrumbs, 4 teaspoons dried mint, 4 teaspoons dried oregano, the grated zest of 1 lemon and 1 crushed garlic clove in a large bowl. Make, chill, and cook the patties as above, then serve stuffed into pittas with hummus and a Greek salad.

chicken with orange & mint

Serves **4**
Preparation time **5 minutes**
Cooking time **15–20 minutes**

salt and **pepper**
4 boneless, skinless **chicken breasts**, about 7 oz each
3 tablespoons **olive oil**
⅔ cup freshly squeezed **orange juice**
1 small **orange**, sliced
2 tablespoons chopped **mint**
1 tablespoon **butter**

Season the chicken breasts to taste with salt and pepper. Heat the oil in a large nonstick skillet, add the chicken breasts, and cook over medium heat, turning once, for 4–5 minutes or until golden all over.

Pour in the orange juice, add the orange slices, and bring to a gentle simmer. Cover tightly, reduce the heat to low, and cook gently for 8–10 minutes or until the chicken is cooked through. Add the chopped mint and butter and stir to mix well. Cook over high heat, stirring, for 2 minutes. Serve immediately.

For chicken with rosemary & lemon, bruise 4 sprigs of rosemary in a mortar and pestle, then chop finely. Put the grated zest and juice of 2 lemons, 3 crushed garlic cloves, 4 tablespoons olive oil, and the rosemary in a nonmetallic dish. Add the chicken breasts and mix to coat thoroughly. Cover and leave to marinate in the refrigerator until required. Cook the chicken breasts in a preheated hot ridged griddle pan for 5 minutes on each side or until cooked through.

lamb with tangy lima beans

Serves **2**
Preparation time **10 minutes**
Cooking time **10 minutes**

2 tablespoons finely chopped
  mint
1 tablespoon finely chopped
  thyme
1 tablespoon finely chopped
  oregano
½ tablespoon finely chopped
  rosemary
4 teaspoons **wholegrain
  mustard**
4 **lamb cutlets**, about
  4 oz each

Tangy lima beans
2 teaspoons **vegetable oil**
1 **onion**, chopped
1 tablespoon **tomato paste**
¼ cup **pineapple juice**
2 tablespoons **lemon juice**
a few drops of **Tabasco sauce**
8 oz canned **lima beans**,
  drained
pepper

Mix together all the chopped herbs on a plate. Spread mustard on both sides of each noisette, then press into the herb mixture to coat evenly.

Make the tangy lima beans. Heat the oil in a skillet, add the onion, and fry gently for 5 minutes. Add the remaining ingredients and cook gently for 5 minutes.

Meanwhile, secure the thin end of the lamb around the base with a toothpick. Place on a foil-lined broiler rack and cook under a preheated hot broiler for 4 minutes on each side or until cooked but still slightly pink in the center. Serve immediately, surrounded by the tangy lima beans and accompanied by mixed salad leaves, if liked.

For lamb noisettes wrapped in prosciutto, mix together 1 tablespoon finely chopped drained capers, 1 crushed garlic clove, ½ tablespoon chopped rosemary, the grated zest of ½ lemon, and 1 tablespoon olive oil in a nonmetallic shallow dish. Add the lamb noisettes and toss to coat in the marinade. Season well, cover, and leave to marinate in the refrigerator for at least 20 minutes. Fold 4 slices of prosciutto lengthways, then wrap around the edge of each of the noisettes. Heat 1 tablespoon vegetable oil in an ovenproof skillet and brown the prosciutto edges of the noisettes, then seal each side of the lamb briefly. Cook in a preheated oven, 400°F, for 12–15 minutes or until cooked but still slightly pink in the center. Remove from the oven and leave to rest. Serve with wilted spinach and crushed garlicky potatoes.

beef strips with radicchio

Serves **4**
Preparation time **5 minutes**
Cooking time **5 minutes**

3 **sirloin steaks**, about
   10 oz each
½ tablespoon **olive oil**
2 **garlic cloves**, finely chopped
5 oz **radicchio**, sliced into
   1 inch strips
salt

Trim the fat from the steaks and slice the meat into very thin strips.

Heat the oil in a heavy-based skillet over high heat, add the garlic and steak strips, season with salt, and stir-fry for 2 minutes or until the steak strips are golden brown.

Add the radicchio and stir-fry until the leaves are just beginning to wilt. Serve immediately.

For beef & caramelized onion couscous salad, brush 1½ lb beef fillet with 1 tablespoon olive oil, then sprinkle well with pepper. Heat a nonstick skillet over medium-high heat and cook the beef for 4 minutes on each side or until seared all over but still rare inside. Remove from the pan and leave to rest. To make the onion couscous, heat 2 tablespoons olive oil in the skillet over medium heat, add 4 sliced onions, and fry, stirring occasionally, for 8–10 minutes or until softened. Meanwhile, put 1¼ cups couscous in a heatproof bowl and pour over 2½ cups boiling chicken or beef stock. Cover and leave to stand for 5 minutes or according to the package instructions, until the stock has been absorbed, then fluff up with a fork. Mix together 2 tablespoons Dijon mustard, a little olive oil, the juice of 1 lemon, and salt and pepper, and toss with the couscous and onions. Slice the beef and place on top of the couscous. Serve with some arugula as a side dish.

cheat's calzone

Serves **1**
Preparation time **5 minutes**
Cooking time **5 minutes**

2 small **soft flour tortillas**
2 teaspoons **sun-dried tomato paste**
1 **tomato**, sliced
2 **slices bacon**, broiled and chopped
4 slices **Milano salami**, cut into strips
3 oz **mozzarella cheese**, thinly sliced
a few **basil leaves**
4–6 **baby spinach leaves**
1 tablespoon **olive oil**
salt and **pepper**

Rinse one side of each tortilla with water to soften, then spread tomato paste over the dampened side and layer the tomato paste, bacon, salami, and mozzarella on top. Add the basil leaves and spinach and a little salt and pepper.

Fold each tortilla over the filling and press the edges together (don't worry if the edges don't stick together in places). Brush the dry outsides of the tortillas with oil and cook in a ridged grddle pan or skillet for 1–2 minutes on each side or until golden. Cut in half and serve immediately.

For cheese & ham calzone, prepare the tortillas as above and spread with 2 teaspoons pesto instead of the tomato paste. Layer 2 slices of ham, chopped, ½ cup thinly sliced mushrooms, and 3 oz grated or sliced Cheddar cheese on top and season with salt and pepper. Fold over and cook the tortillas as above.

jerk chicken wings

Serves **4**
Preparation time **5 minutes**,
   plus marinating
Cooking time **12 minutes**

12 large **chicken wings**
2 tablespoons **olive oil**
1 tablespoon **jerk seasoning
   mix**
juice of ½ **lemon**
1 teaspoon **salt**
chopped **parsley**, to garnish
lemon wedges, to serve

Put the chicken wings in a nonmetallic dish. Whisk together the oil, jerk seasoning mix, lemon juice, and salt in a small bowl. Pour over the wings and stir well until evenly coated. Cover and leave to marinate in the refrigerator for at least 30 minutes or overnight.

Arrange the chicken wings on a broiler rack and cook under a preheated broiler, basting halfway through cooking with any remaining marinade, for 6 minutes on each side or until cooked through, tender, and lightly charred at the edges. Increase or reduce the temperature setting of the broiler, if necessary, to make sure that the wings cook through.

Sprinkle with the chopped parsley and serve immediately with lemon wedges for squeezing over.

For jerk lamb kebabs, coat 1 ½ lb boneless lamb, cut into bite-sized pieces, in the jerk marinade as above, leaving to marinate overnight if time allows. Thread the meat onto 8 skewers and cook under a preheated broiler or on a barbecue for 6–8 minutes on each side or until cooked to your liking.

polenta with parma ham & cheese

Serves **4**
Preparation time **10 minutes**
Cooking time **15 minutes**

4 cups **water**
2 cups **instant polenta**
8 oz **asparagus spears**,
   trimmed
6 slices of **Parma ham**
3½ oz **fontina cheese**, sliced
2 tablespoons grated
   Parmesan cheese
salt and **pepper**
basil leaves, to garnish
   (optional)

Measure the water into a large heavy-based saucepan and bring to a boil. Put the polenta in a large measuring cup and pour into the water in a slow but steady stream, stirring vigorously with a wooden spoon to stop any lumps from forming. Reduce the heat to a gentle simmer and cook, stirring continuously, for about 5 minutes or until the polenta is thick and comes away from the side of the pan. Season with salt and pepper.

Pour the polenta into a greased baking dish about 10 x 7 inches. Blanch the asparagus in a saucepan of boiling water for 1–2 minutes or until just tender. Drain well. Top the polenta with a layer of ham, then the asparagus, and, lastly, a layer of fontina and Parmesan.

Cook under a preheated very hot broiler, about 3 inches from the heat, until crisp and golden. Scatter basil leaves over the top, cut into wedges, and serve immediately.

For polenta with meaty mushrooms, cook the polenta and pour into a baking dish as above. Heat 2 tablespoons olive oil in a skillet, add 10 oz sausagemeat and fry until browned. Add 2 oz reconstituted dried porcini mushrooms, 1½ cups thinly sliced cup mushrooms, 2 chopped garlic cloves, and the finely chopped leaves from 2 sprigs of rosemary. Spread the meaty mushroom mixture over the top of the polenta, cut into wedges, and serve immediately.

lamb cutlets with mojo sauce

Serves **4**
Preparation time **10 minutes**
Cooking time **10 minutes**

8 small **lamb cutlets**
1 **garlic clove**, crushed
1 tablespoon chopped **thyme**
3 tablespoons **olive oil**
1 lb 2 oz **baby new potatoes**,
    scrubbed and thickly sliced
    salt and **pepper**

Sauce
2 **red chilies**, seeded and
    chopped
4 **garlic cloves**, roughly
    chopped
2 teaspoons **cumin seeds**,
    crushed
small handful of **fresh cilantro
    leaves**
4 tablespoons **olive oil**
1 tablespoon **sherry vinegar**

Trim the lamb cutlets of most of the fat, scraping
it away completely from the tips of the bones.
Mix together the garlic, thyme, oil, and a little salt
and pepper in a bowl, then spread over the lamb.

Make the sauce. Put the chilies, garlic, cumin seeds,
cilantro, and oil in a food processor or blender and blend
to a thin paste. Stir in the vinegar and season with
a little salt.

Cook the baby new potatoes in a saucepan of boiling,
salted water for 10 minutes until tender.

Meanwhile, heat a griddle pan or heavy-based skillet,
add the lamb and fry for about 4 minutes on each side
or until cooked but still slightly pink in the center. Cook
for longer if you prefer them cooked through.

Drain the potatoes and tip them back into the pan. Add
half the sauce, toss to coat, then transfer the remaining
sauce to a small dish.

Transfer the potatoes to 4 warmed plates. Place
2 lamb cutlets on top, and serve the remaining sauce
separately for drizzling over the cutlets.

For lamb with spring-green sauce, prepare and
cook the lamb as above. Put a handful of watercress,
the juice of ½ lemon and ½ cup melted butter in a food
processor or blender and whizz until combined. Drizzle
the sauce over the cooked lamb and serve immediately.

thai red pork & bean curry

Serves **4**
Preparation time **10 minutes**
Cooking time **5 minutes**

2 tablespoons **peanut oil**
1½ tablespoons **Thai red curry paste**
12 oz **lean pork**, sliced into thin strips
⅔ cup **green beans**, trimmed and cut in half
2 tablespoons **Thai fish sauce**
1 teaspoon **superfine sugar**
Chinese chives or **regular chives**, to garnish

Heat the oil in a wok or large skillet over medium heat until the oil starts to shimmer, add the curry paste, and cook, stirring, until it releases its aroma.

Add the pork and beans and stir-fry for 2–3 minutes or until the meat is cooked through and the beans are just tender.

Stir in the fish sauce and sugar and serve, garnished with Chinese chives or regular chives.

For chicken green curry with sugar snap peas, replace the red curry paste with 1½ tablespoons green curry paste (see page 94), the pork with 12 oz sliced chicken breast and the green beans with 1 cup sliced sugar snap peas. Cook as above, adding a squeeze of lime juice before serving.

duck with honey & lime sauce

Serves **4**

Preparation time **10 minutes**

Cooking time **10 minutes**

4 **duck breasts**, about 7 oz
  each
3 tablespoons **liquid honey**
½ cup **white wine**
finely grated zest of **1 lime**
⅓ cup **lime juice**
scant ½ cup **chicken stock**
1 tablespoon peeled and finely
  chopped **fresh ginger root**
½ teaspoon **arrowroot**
  (optional)
1 tablespoon **water**
salt and **pepper**

Score the skin of each duck breast through to the flesh 4 times and rub generously with salt and pepper. Heat a heavy-based skillet or ridged griddle pan until hot, add the duck breasts, skin-side down, and cook for 3 minutes or until the skin is crisp. Drain off all the fat from the pan.

Transfer the duck to a roasting pan, skin-side down, and brush with 1 tablespoon of the honey. Roast in a preheated oven, 400°F, for 5 minutes or until cooked but still slightly pink inside. Remove from the oven and leave to rest for 3 minutes, then slice diagonally.

Meanwhile, add the wine, lime zest and juice, stock, ginger, and remaining honey to the skillet, bring to a boil, and cook for 5 minutes. If using, blend the arrowroot with the measurement water in a cup and add to the sauce. Return to a boil, stirring continuously, and cook until thickened. Serve the duck with steamed chantenay carrots, sugar snap peas, and asparagus, with the sauce drizzled over the top of the duck.

For French-style duck with orange, prepare the duck breasts as above, then put in a hot skillet, not a griddle pan, and cook as above. Transfer to a roasting pan, omit the honey, and cook as above. Meanwhile, peel 2 oranges, slice in rounds, and set aside. Put ½ cup orange juice, 1 tablespoon balsamic vinegar, 1 tablespoon superfine sugar and 1 tablespoon cornflour mixed with a little water into the skillet, bring to a boil, and stir until thickened, then pour in 2 tablespoons Grand Marnier. Spoon over the sliced duck and serve with the orange slices.

red hot hamburgers

Serves **4**
Preparation time **10 minutes**
Cooking time **8–16 minutes**

1 ¼ lb **ground beef**
2 **garlic cloves**, crushed
1 **red onion**, finely chopped
1 **red chili**, seeded and finely
chopped
1 bunch of **parsley**, chopped
1 tablespoon **Worcestershire
sauce**
1 **egg**, beaten
4 **hamburger buns**, split
spicy salad leaves, such as
arugula or **mizuna greens**
1 **beefsteak tomato**, sliced
salt and **pepper**

Put the beef in a large bowl, add the garlic, onion, chili, parsley, Worcestershire sauce, egg, and a little salt and pepper and mix well.

Heat a ridged griddle pan until smoking hot. Divide the meat mixture into 4 and shape into patties. Add them to the pan and cook for 3 minutes on each side for rare, 5 minutes on each side for medium, or 7 minutes on each side for well done. Remove from the pan, cover in foil to keep warm, and leave to rest while you griddle the buns.

Wash and dry the pan, then reheat, add the bun halves, and cook briefly on the sliced side until lightly charred. Fill each bun with some salad leaves, a slice of tomato, and a beef patty. Serve immediately with the condiment of your choice.

For aromatic spiced burgers, omit the parsley and Worcestershire sauce from the hamburger mix and replace with 1 tablespoon ground coriander, 1 tablespoon ground cumin, and 1 heaping teaspoon Dijon mustard.

sherried chicken stroganoff

Serves **4**
Preparation time **10 minutes**
Cooking time about **10
  minutes**

2 tablespoons **butter**
2 tablespoons **sunflower oil**
4 boneless, skinless **chicken
  breasts** about 5 oz each,
  cut into long, thin slices
2 **onions**, thinly sliced
1 teaspoon **paprika**
2 teaspoons **mild mustard**
⅓ cup **dry** or **medium dry
  sherry**
⅓ cup **water**
⅓ cup **sour cream**
salt and **pepper**

Heat the butter and oil in a large skillet, add the chicken and onions, and sauté over medium heat for 6–7 minutes or until the chicken and onions are a deep golden color.

Stir in the paprika, then add the mustard, sherry, measurement water, and salt and pepper.

Cook for 2–3 minutes or until the chicken is cooked through, then add the cream and swirl together. Spoon onto plates and serve with rice and green string beans, if liked.

For chicken & fennel stroganoff, fry the sliced chicken breasts in the butter and oil as above, replacing one of the onions with 1 small, thinly sliced fennel bulb. When golden, omit the paprika and add the mustard and ⅓ cup Pernod, instead of the sherry, igniting it with a match. Add the measurement water and salt and pepper as above. Cook for 2–3 minutes or until the chicken is cooked through, then add ⅓ cup crème fraîche and stir until just melted. Serve as above.

chicken wrapped in parma ham

Serves **4**
Preparation time **10 minutes**
Cooking time **10 minutes**

4 boneless, skinless **chicken breasts**, about 5 oz each
4 slices of **Parma ham**
4 **sage leaves**
all-purpose flour, for dusting
2 tablespoons **butter**
2 tablespoons **olive oil**
4 stems **cherry tomatoes on the vine**
⅔ cup **dry white wine**
salt and **pepper**

Lay each chicken breast between 2 sheets of plastic wrap and flatten with a rolling pin until wafer thin. Season with salt and pepper.

Set a slice of Parma ham on each chicken breast, followed by a sage leaf. Secure the sage and ham in position with a toothpick, then lightly dust both sides of the chicken with flour. Season again with salt and pepper.

Heat the butter and oil in a large skillet over high heat, add the chicken, and cook for 4–5 minutes on each side or until the juices run clear when pierced with a knife. Add the tomatoes and wine to the pan and bubble until the wine has thickened and reduced by about half. Serve immediately, accompanied by a green salad.

For veal escalopes with rosemary & pancetta, take 4 veal escalopes, about 5 oz each, and flatten as above. Top each flattened escalope with a scattering of rosemary leaves, then wrap each in a slice of pancetta, instead of the Parma ham, omitting the sage. Dust with flour, season with salt and pepper, and cook as above.

taverna-style broiled lamb with feta

Serves **4**
Preparation time **8 minutes**
Cooking time **6–8 minutes**

1 lb leg or shoulder of **lamb**,
  diced

Marinade
2 tablespoons chopped
  oregano
1 tablespoon chopped
  rosemary
grated zest of **1 lemon**
2 tablespoons olive oil
salt and **pepper**

Feta salad
7 oz **feta cheese**, sliced
1 tablespoon chopped
  oregano
2 tablespoons chopped
  parsley
grated zest and juice of
  1 lemon
½ small **red onion**, finely sliced
3 tablespoons **olive oil**

Mix together the marinade ingredients in a nonmetallic bowl, then add the lamb and mix to coat thoroughly. Thread the meat onto 4 skewers.

Arrange the sliced feta on a large serving dish and sprinkle over the herbs, lemon zest, and sliced onion. Drizzle over the lemon juice and oil and season with salt and pepper.

Cook the lamb skewers under a preheated hot broiler or in a griddle pan, turning frequently, for 6–8 minutes or until browned and almost cooked through. Remove from the broiler or pan and leave to rest for 1–2 minutes.

Serve the lamb, with any pan juices poured over, with the salad and accompanied with plenty of crusty bread, if liked.

For pork with red cabbage, replace the lamb with 1 lb lean, boneless pork, diced. Marinate and cook the pork as above. Replace the feta with 2 cups finely chopped red cabbage. Omit the oregano and replace the lemon with an orange. Mix the salad ingredients together and leave to marinate for 5 minutes before serving.

chicken livers with marsala & raisins

Serves **4**
Preparation time **10 minutes**
Cooking time about **10 minutes**

13 oz fresh **chicken livers**
2 tablespoons **butter**
2 tablespoons **olive oil**
¼ cup **raisins**
⅓ cup **Marsala**
squeeze of **lemon juice**
salt and **pepper**
plenty of chopped **chives**, to garnish

Rinse the livers and pat them dry on paper towels. Slice each into about 4 pieces, cutting out and discarding any white parts. Season with salt and pepper.

Heat the butter and oil in a skillet. When it is very hot, add the livers and fry them quickly, turning them so they brown evenly, for 5 minutes or until golden. If you prefer the livers well done, fry them for a further couple of minutes. Add the raisins and fry for 1 minute. Remove the livers and raisins with a slotted spoon and keep warm.

Add the Marsala to the pan and bring to a boil. Cook for a couple of minutes until syrupy, then stir in the lemon juice. Pour the sauce over the livers and serve scattered with chives.

For rustic chicken livers, heat the butter in a skillet, add 1 thinly sliced onion and 5 oz chopped bacon and fry for 5–6 minutes or until the bacon is getting crisp and the onion has softened. Add the prepared chicken livers and cook as above, omitting the raisins. Remove with a slotted spoon and keep warm. Add ¼ cup all-purpose flour to the pan juices, then slowly stir in ⅓ cup red wine to make a smooth sauce. Pour over the livers, bacon, and onion and serve immediately.

indonesian beef strips

Serves **4**
Preparation time **5 minutes**
Cooking time **8 minutes**

1 **onion**, roughly chopped
2 **garlic cloves**, peeled
1 inch piece of fresh **ginger root**, peeled and sliced
1 **red chili**, seeded
2 tablespoons **dried shrimp**
3 tablespoons **peanut oil**
1 lb **lean beef,** cut into thin strips
1 tablespoon **tamarind paste**
2 tablespoons **dark soy sauce**
4 tablespoons **water**
1 teaspoon **Demerara sugar**
small handful of **mint leaves**, shredded, plus extra whole ones to garnish
salt and **pepper**
1 tablespoon **snipped chives**, to garnish

Put the onion, garlic, ginger, chili, and dried shrimp in a food processor or blender and blend until it forms a smooth paste.

Heat the oil in a wok or large skillet over medium heat, add the paste and cook, stirring continuously, for about 2 minutes or until the oil separates from the other ingredients.

Add the beef and stir-fry until the meat turns opaque, then add the tamarind paste, soy sauce, and the water. Simmer, uncovered, for 2–3 minutes or until most of the liquid has evaporated and the meat is tender.

Stir in the sugar and shredded mint leaves, season to taste with salt and pepper, and garnish with chives and a few whole mint leaves. Serve with a vegetable dish and rice, if liked.

For pork with yellow bell peppers & mushrooms, replace the beef with 1 lb lean pork, cut into thin strips, and add 1 yellow bell pepper, cored, seeded, and cut into thin strips, and 1 cup halved chestnut mushrooms. Follow the recipe as above, adding the additional vegetables to the wok or pan with the meat.

griddled salsa chicken

Serves 4
Preparation time **10 minutes**
Cooking time **6 minutes**

4 boneless **chicken breasts**,
    skin on, about 5 oz each
3 tablespoons **olive oil**
salt and **pepper**

Salsa
1 **red onion**, finely chopped
2 **tomatoes**, seeded and
    diced
1 **cucumber**, finely diced
1 **red chili**, seeded and finely
    chopped
small handful of **fresh cilantro
    leaves**, chopped
juice of 1 **lime**

Remove the skin from the chicken breasts. Using kitchen scissors or poultry shears, cut each breast in half lengthways but without cutting all the way through. Open each breast out flat. Brush with the oil and season well with salt and pepper.

Heat a ridged griddle pan until very hot, add the chicken breasts, and cook for 3 minutes on each side or until cooked through and griddle-marked.

Meanwhile, make the salsa. Mix together the onion, tomatoes, cucumber, red chili, cilantro, and lime juice. Season well with salt and pepper.

Serve the chicken hot with the spicy salsa spooned over and around.

For griddled tuna with pineapple salsa, prepare and cook 4 thick fresh tuna steaks, about 6 oz each, as for the butterflied chicken breasts above. Meanwhile, in a bowl, mix together ⅓ cup roughly diced drained canned pineapple, 1 finely chopped red onion, 1 tablespoon peeled and finely chopped fresh ginger root, 1 seeded and finely chopped red chili, the grated zest and juice of 1 lime, 2 teaspoons liquid honey, and salt and pepper to taste. Serve the pineapple salsa with the griddled tuna.

deviled tenderloin steaks

Serves **4**

Preparation time **10 minutes**

Cooking time **10 minutes**

2 tablespoons **olive oil**

4 **tenderloin steaks**, about
6 oz each

2 tablespoons **balsamic
vinegar**

⅓ cup **full-bodied red wine**

4 tablespoons **beef stock**

2 **garlic cloves**, chopped

1 teaspoon crushed **fennel
seeds**

1 tablespoon **sun-dried
tomato paste**

½ teaspoon crushed **dried
chilies**

salt and **pepper**

chopped **flat-leaf parsley**, to
garnish

Heat the oil in a nonstick skillet until smoking hot, add
the steaks, and cook over very high heat for about 2
minutes on each side, if you want your steaks to be
medium rare. Remove from the skillet, season with salt
and pepper, and keep warm.

Pour the vinegar, wine, and stock into the skillet and
boil for 30 seconds, scraping any sediment from the
bottom of the skillet. Add the garlic and fennel seeds,
then whisk in the sun-dried tomato paste and crushed
chilies. Bring the sauce to a boil, then boil fast to reduce
down until syrupy.

Transfer the steaks to warmed serving plates, pouring
any collected meat juices into the sauce. Return the
sauce to a boil, then season with salt and pepper.

Slice the steaks before serving, if you wish. Pour the
sauce over the steaks and serve immediately, garnished
with chopped parsley.

For deviled chicken breasts, heat the oil as above and
cook 4 boneless, skinless chicken breasts for 5 minutes
on each side or until cooked through. Leaving the
chicken in the pan, follow the recipe above, replacing
the beef stock with ¼ cup chicken stock and using
½ teaspoon dried oregano instead of the fennel seeds.

fish & seafood

galician-style monkfish

Serves **4**
Preparation time **10 minutes**
Cooking time **10 minutes**

15 whole **blanched almonds**
1 lb 10 oz **monkfish fillet**,
  skinned
1 **onion**, thinly sliced
olive oil, for drizzling
3 **garlic cloves**, crushed
large pinch of **saffron threads**,
  crushed
1 tablespoon finely chopped
  parsley
1²⁄₃ cups cups fresh or frozen
  peas
salt and **pepper**

Roast the almonds in a dry skillet over medium heat for a few minutes until toasted.

Cut the monkfish into 8 evenly sized pieces. Spread the onion over the base of a medium-sized dutch oven and arrange the monkfish on top of them. Season to taste with salt and pepper and drizzle over a little oil. Cover tightly and cook over medium heat for 5–6 minutes.

Meanwhile, in a food processor add the almonds, garlic, saffron, and parsley, and blitz until finely chopped. Add 2–3 tablespoons water and blitz again to make a coarse paste.

Remove the lid from the dutch oven, spread the almond mixture over the top of the fish, and add the peas. Cover and cook for a further 4–5 minutes or until the fish is cooked through. Serve immediately.

For monkfish wrapped in Parma ham, prepare the monkfish as above and wrap each piece in a slice of Parma ham, then season with pepper. Heat 1 tablespoon olive oil in a skillet, add the monkfish, and fry for 2–3 minutes on each side or until browned. Place in a roasting pan and cook in a preheated oven, 425°F, for 8 minutes or until cooked through. Remove from the oven and leave to rest for 5 minutes. Heat 1 tablespoon olive oil in the pan, add 1 chopped onion and 2 crushed garlic cloves, and fry gently until softened. Add 1 lb cherry tomatoes and a handful of chopped basil and stir together well. Serve the monkfish on a bed of wilted spinach leaves with the tomatoes.

lime & coconut squid

Serves **2**
Preparation time **15 minutes**
Cooking time **5 minutes**

10–12 prepared **baby squid**,
    about 12 oz including
    tentacles, cleaned
4 **limes**, halved

Dressing
2 **red chilies**, seeded and
    finely chopped
finely grated zest and juice of
    2 **limes**
1 inch piece of **fresh ginger
    root**, peeled and grated
¾ cup freshly grated **coconut**
4 tablespoons **peanut oil**
1–2 tablespoons **chili oil**
1 tablespoon **white wine
    vinegar**

Cut down the side of each squid so they can be laid flat on a cutting board. Using a sharp knife, lightly score the inside flesh in a criss-cross pattern.

Mix all the dressing ingredients together in a bowl. Toss the squid in half of the dressing until thoroughly coated.

Heat a ridged griddle pan until smoking hot, add the limes, cut-side down, and cook for 2 minutes or until well charred. Remove from the pan and set aside. Keeping the griddle pan very hot, add the squid pieces, and cook for 1 minute. Turn them over and cook for a further minute or until they turn white, lose their transparency, and are charred.

Transfer the squid to a cutting board and cut into strips. Drizzle with the remaining dressing and serve immediately with the charred limes and a salad of mixed green leaves.

For lemon & garlic squid, remove the tentacles from the prepared squid and slice the bodies into rings. Place in a nonmetallic dish with the juice of 1 lemon and leave to marinate for 5 minutes. Heat ⅓ cup olive oil in a large skillet and add 3 chopped garlic cloves and the grated zest of 1 lemon. When the oil is very hot, add the squid and cook over high heat for 1–2 minutes or until it turns white and loses its transparency. Season with salt and pepper and serve sprinkled with chopped parsley and lemon wedges.

sugar & spice salmon

Serves **4**
Preparation time **5 minutes**
Cooking time **10 minutes**

4 **salmon fillets**, about
   7 oz each
3 tablespoons **light
   muscovado sugar**
2 **garlic cloves**, crushed
1 teaspoon **cumin seeds**,
   crushed
1 teaspoon smoked or ordinary
   paprika
1 tablespoon **white wine
   vinegar**
3 tablespoons **peanut oil**
salt and **pepper**
½ teaspoon **cumin seeds**,
   crushed
2 **zucchini**, sliced into thin
   ribbons
lemon or **lime slices**, to serve

Put the salmon fillets in a lightly oiled roasting pan.
Mix together the sugar, garlic, cumin seeds, paprika,
vinegar, and a little salt in a bowl, then spread the
mixture all over the fish so that it is thinly coated.
Drizzle with 1 tablespoon of oil.

Bake in a preheated oven, 425°F, for 10 minutes or
until the fish is cooked through.

Heat the remaining oil in a large skillet, add the crushed
cumin seeds, and fry for 10 seconds. Add the zucchini
ribbons, season with salt and pepper, and stir-fry for
2–3 minutes until just softened.

Transfer to warm serving plates and serve the salmon
on top, garnished with lemon or lime wedges.

For salmon with pesto crust, put the salmon in
a lightly oiled roasting pan, season with pepper,
and add a squeeze of lemon juice. Mix together
4 tablespoons pesto and 2 handfuls of fresh white
breadcrumbs in a bowl, then spread on top of the
salmon. Grate Parmesan cheese over the top and
drizzle with olive oil. Bake as above and serve with
green beans and new potatoes.

skate with balsamic butter

Serves **2**
Preparation time **5 minutes**
Cooking time **15 minutes**

2 teaspoons **plain flour**
2 **skate wings**, about
7 oz each
scant ¼ cup **butter**
3 tablespoons **balsamic
vinegar**
1 tablespoon **capers**, drained
salt and **pepper**

Mix the flour with a little salt and pepper and use it to dust the skate wings.

Heat a knob of the butter in a large skillet, add the skate, and fry gently for about 5 minutes on each side or until cooked through. Remove with a slotted spoon and keep warm on serving plates.

Add the remaining butter, balsamic vinegar, and capers to the skillet and cook over medium heat, whisking until bubbling and syrupy. Season to taste with salt and pepper, then pour over the skate. Serve immediately with boiled baby new potatoes tossed in chopped parsley and a side salad.

For skate wings with lime & cilantro tartare sauce, first make the tartare sauce. Break 1 egg into the bowl of a food processor, add ½ teaspoon sea salt, 1 peeled garlic clove, and ½ teaspoon mustard powder, then switch the motor on and pour ¾ cup olive oil through the feed tube in a thin, steady stream. When all the oil has been added and the sauce has thickened, add 1 scant tablespoon lime juice, 1 tablespoon drained capers, 4 cornichons, 1 tablespoon chopped cilantro, and some pepper. Pulse until the ingredients are chopped. Cook the skate in a knob of butter as above and serve with the sauce.

clams with tomatoes

Serves **4**
Preparation time **10 minutes**
Cooking time **10 minutes**

2 tablespoons **olive oil**
3 **garlic cloves**, finely chopped
2 ri**pe tomatoes**, finely
  chopped
2 lb live **clams**, cleaned
½ cup **Manzanilla sherry**
4 tablespoons finely chopped
  parsley
salt and **pepper**

Heat the oil in a large skillet, add the garlic and tomatoes, and cook over medium heat, stirring, for 3–4 minutes.

Discard any clams that won't shut when tapped, then add them to the pan with the sherry and parsley. Season to taste with salt and pepper, then cover tightly and cook over high heat, shaking the pan vigorously several times, for 4–5 minutes or until the clams have opened. Discard any that remain closed.

Serve the clams immediately in their cooking liquid or leave to cool to room temperature.

For linguine alle vongole, prepare the clams as above. Cook 13 oz dried linguine in a large saucepan of salted boiling water according to the package instructions until al dente. Meanwhile, heat 1 tablespoon olive oil in a large saucepan, add 1 chopped garlic clove and 1 crumbled dried chili and cook until softened. Add the clams and increase the heat to high, then add ½ cup vermouth and cover tightly. Cook as above, discarding any clams that remain closed. Drain the pasta, add to the clams, and toss well. Stir through some chopped parsley and serve immediately.

tuna steaks with green salsa

Serves **4**
Preparation time **15 minutes**,
 plus marinating
Cooking time **2–4 minutes**

2 tablespoons **olive oil**
grated zest of **1 lemon**
2 teaspoons chopped **parsley**
½ teaspoon crushed
 coriander seeds
4 fresh **tuna steaks**, about
 5 oz each
salt and **pepper**

Salsa
2 tablespoons **capers**, drained
 and chopped
2 tablespoons chopped
 cornichons
1 tablespoon finely chopped
 parsley
2 teaspoons chopped **chives**
2 teaspoons finely chopped
 chervil
heaping ¼ cup pitted **green
 olives**, chopped
1 **shallot,** finely chopped
 (optional)
2 tablespoons **lemon juice**
2 tablespoons **olive oil**

Mix together the oil, lemon zest, parsley, and coriander seeds with plenty of pepper in a nonmetallic dish. Add the tuna steaks and coat evenly with the mixture. Leave to marinate while you make the salsa.

Make the salsa by mixing together all the ingredients in a bowl. Season to taste with salt and pepper and set aside for the flavors to infuse.

Heat a ridged griddle pan or skillet until hot, add the tuna steaks, and cook for 1–2 minutes on each side or until seared all over. The tuna should be well seared but rare. Remove from the pan and leave to rest for 2–3 minutes.

Serve the tuna steaks with a spoonful of salsa, a dressed salad, and plenty of fresh crusty bread.

For yellow bell pepper & mustard salsa, to serve as an alternative accompaniment, mix together in a bowl 2 cored, seeded, and finely chopped yellow bell peppers, 1 tablespoon Dijon mustard, 2 tablespoons each finely chopped chives, parsley, and dill, 1 teaspoon sugar, 1 tablespoon cider vinegar, and 2 tablespoons olive oil.

scallops with citrus dressing

Serves **4**
Preparation time **10 minutes**
Cooking time **10 minutes**

16 raw **jumbo shrimp**
24 **fresh scallops**, roe
  removed
1 large, ripe but firm **mango**,
  peeled, seeded, and cut into
  chunks
2 tablespoons **oil**, for frying
4 cups **mixed salad leaves**

Citrus dressing
juice of ½ **pink grapefruit**
finely grated zest and juice of
  1 **lime**
1 teaspoon **liquid honey**
1 tablespoon **raspberry**
  vinegar
⅓ cup **lemon oil**

Make the citrus dressing by mixing together all the ingredients in a small bowl.

Poach the shrimps in a saucepan of simmering water for 2 minutes or until they turn pink. Drain well.

Put the scallops, mango, and shrimp in a bowl and pour over 3 tablespoons of the dressing. Mix well to coat, then thread them alternately onto 8 skewers.

Heat the oil in a large skillet over medium heat, add the skewers, and fry, turning and basting occasionally, for about 5–7 minutes or until golden brown and cooked through.

Arrange the skewers on plates with the salad leaves and serve with the remaining dressing.

For haloumi & mango kebabs with citrus dressing, replace the scallops and shrimp with 14½ oz–1 lb haloumi cheese, cut into cubes. Coat with the dressing, thread onto skewers with the mango, and fry as above. Alternatively, cook on a barbecue for about 5–7 minutes or until slightly charred.

griddled red snapper with spinach

Serves **4**
Preparation time **5 minutes**
Cooking time **8 minutes**

4 **red snapper fillets**, about
  6 oz each
½ pound **baby leaf spinach**
1 teaspoon **pumpkin seeds**
1 teaspoon **sunflower seeds**
2 teaspoons **olive oil**
1 bunch of **scallions**,
  shredded, to garnish

Heat a griddle pan over medium heat, add the snapper fillets, and cook for 4 minutes on each side or until cooked through and the fish flakes easily when pressed with a fork.

Meanwhile, steam the spinach until just tender. Drain well, then mix the pumpkin seeds, sunflower seeds, and oil with the spinach in a bowl. Serve immediately with the snapper fillets on top, garnished with the shredded scallions.

For griddled red snapper with couscous, put 1½ cups couscous in a heatproof bowl and pour over 1¼ cups boiling vegetable stock. Cover and leave to stand for 8 minutes or according to the package instructions, until the stock has been absorbed, then fluff up with a fork. Drain 8 oz mixed roasted bell peppers in oil (no need to chop them up) and mix with 1 tablespoon ground cumin, 1 tablespoon ground coriander seeds, and 1 tablespoon olive oil. Then mix into the couscous. Cook the snapper fillets as above and serve on a bed of couscous, sprinkled with the shredded scallions.

shrimp with garlicky beans

Serves **4**
Preparation time **10 minutes**
Cooking time **10 minutes**

4 tablespoons **olive oil**
1 large **onion**, finely chopped
3 **garlic cloves**, crushed
2 x 13 oz cans **cannellini, haricot,** or **lima beans**, drained
½ cup **vegetable** or **fish stock**
13 oz **raw peeled shrimp**
½ teaspoon **mild sweet paprika**
2 tablespoons **sun-dried tomato paste**
1 tablespoon chopped **oregano**
2 teaspoons **liquid honey**
pepper

Heat 2 tablespoons of the oil in a saucepan, add the onion, and fry gently for 5 minutes. Add the garlic and fry for a further minute.

Remove the pan from the heat. Tip in the beans and use a potato masher to crush them. Add the stock and plenty of pepper and set aside.

Dust the shrimp with the paprika and a little salt. Heat the remaining oil in a skillet, add the shrimp, and fry for 5–6 minutes, turning once or twice during cooking, until they turn pink and are cooked through. Stir in the tomato paste, oregano, honey, and 2 tablespoons water and cook for 2–3 minutes or until it begins to bubble.

Meanwhile, reheat the pan with the beans until piping hot. Spoon the bean mixture into small dishes, pile the shrimp on top, and pour over the cooking juices.

For blackened cod with garlicky beans, prepare and cook the beans as above. Spread one side of each of 4 x 6oz cod fillets with 1 heaped teaspoon of ready-made black olive tapenade. Heat 2 tablespoons olive oil in a griddle pan over medium heat, add the fish, and cook for about 5 minutes on each side or until cooked through. Serve on a bed of crushed beans, sprinkled with chopped black olives and parsley.

pasta, crab & arugula salad

Serves **1**
Preparation time **5 minutes,**
  plus cooling
Cooking time **10 minutes**

2 oz dried **pasta,** such as
  rigatoni
grated zest and juice of
  ½ **lime**
2 tablespoons **crème fraîche**
3¼ oz can **crab meat,** drained
8 **cherry tomatoes,** halved
handful of **arugula**

Cook the pasta in a saucepan of boiling water
according to the package instructions until al dente.
Drain well and leave to cool.

Mix together the lime zest and juice, crème fraîche,
and crab meat in a large bowl. Add the cooled pasta
and mix again.

Add the tomatoes and arugula to the bowl, toss
everything together, and serve.

For pasta salad with tuna & chilli, cook the pasta
as above. Drain a 4½ oz can of tuna and mix through
the cooled pasta. Add 1 seeded and finely chopped
red chili, the grated zest and juice of 1 lemon,
2 tablespoons chopped parsley, a handful of arugula,
and 2 tablespoons olive oil and mix together well.
Season to taste with salt and pepper and serve.

soy & orange salmon with noodles

Serves **4**
Preparation time **5 minutes**
Cooking time **10–15 minutes**

4 skinless **salmon fillets**,
 about 6 oz each
spray **olive oil**, for oiling
8 oz dried **soba noodles**
4 tablespoons **dark soy sauce**
2 tablespoons **orange juice**
2 tablespoons **mirin** (rice wine
 seasoning)
2 teaspoons **sesame oil**
2 tablespoons **sesame seeds**

Remove any bones from the salmon fillets and put
the salmon in a bowl. Heat a heavy-based skillet until
hot and spray lightly with oil. Add the salmon and cook
for 3–4 minutes on each side or until cooked through.
Remove from the pan, wrap loosely in foil, and leave to
rest for 5 minutes.

Meanwhile, cook the noodles in a large saucepan of
boiling water for about 5 minutes, or according to the
package instructions, until just tender.

While the noodles are cooking, mix together the soy
sauce, orange juice, and mirin in a bowl, then pour into
the skillet and bring to a boil. Reduce the heat and
simmer for 1 minute.

Drain the noodles well, return to the pan, and toss with
the sesame oil, then sprinkle over the seeds. Divide the
salmon among 4 serving bowls and top with the sauce.
Serve with steamed sugar snap peas.

For salmon, orange & soy parcels, put each salmon
fillet on a 12 inch square of foil. Draw the foil edges
up to form "cups" and add the soy sauce, orange juice,
and mirin as above, along with 2 sliced scallions,
2 sliced garlic cloves, and 2 teaspoons peeled and
grated fresh ginger root. Seal the edges of the foil
together to form parcels, transfer to a baking pan,
and bake in a preheated oven, 400°F, for 15 minutes.
Remove from the oven and leave to rest briefly, then
serve with steamed rice.

mixed seafood grill

Serves **4**

Preparation time **10 minutes**, plus infusing

Cooking time **10 minutes**

10 oz **ready-prepared squid**, cleaned

12 **raw shrimp**, shells on

12 live **clams**, cleaned

12 live **mussels**, scrubbed and debearded

lemon wedges, to serve

Dressing

2 **garlic cloves**, peeled and bruised

6 tablespoons **extra virgin olive oil**

2 tablespoons chopped **parsley**

Cut down the side of the squid so that it can be laid flat on a cutting board. Using a sharp knife, lightly score the inside flesh in a criss-cross pattern, then cut the squid into 1¼ inch squares. Chill until required.

Make the dressing. Put the garlic in a small bowl, add the oil, and stir in the parsley. Leave the flavors to infuse for at least 15 minutes.

When ready to serve, heat a ridged griddle pan over high heat until searing hot. Lightly brush the shrimp and squid with half the dressing. Add the shrimp to the pan and cook for 3–4 minutes on each side or until they turn pink. Transfer to a warmed serving platter.

Add the squid flesh (but not the tentacles), the clams, and mussels to the pan (discarding any that don't shut when tapped), and cook for 5–7 minutes or until the squid turns white and is charred and the clams and mussels have opened. Discard any that remain closed. Add the squid tentacles and cook for 2–3 minutes more, then transfer everthing to the serving platter and drizzle all the seafood with the remaining dressing. Serve immediately with lemon wedges, avocado dip (see below), and bread, if liked.

For tangy avocado dip to serve as an accompaniment, halve, seed, and peel 2 very ripe, large avocados and put in a food processor or blender with 2 tablespoons good-quality mayonnaise, 2 tablespoons sour cream, the juice of 1 lemon, 1 teaspoon mild chili sauce, if liked, and some salt and pepper. Blend until smooth, spoon into a small bowl, and place on the serving platter.

broiled sardines with tomato salsa

Serves **1**
Preparation time **10 minutes**
Cooking time **3–4 minutes**

3 **fresh sardines**, about
   4 oz in total, gutted
4 tablespoons **lemon juice**
1 tablespoon chopped **basil**
salt and **pepper**

Tomato salsa
8 **cherry tomatoes**, chopped
1 **scallion**, sliced
1 tablespoon chopped **basil**
½ **red bell pepper**, cored,
   seeded, and chopped

Make the tomato salsa by mixing together all the ingredients in a bowl.

Put the sardines on a broiler pan and drizzle with the lemon juice. Season to taste with salt and pepper. Cook the sardines under a preheated hot broiler, turning once, for 3–4 minutes or until cooked through.

Sprinkle with the chopped basil and serve immediately with the tomato salsa and toasted ciabatta.

For quick sardine & anchovy toast, cook the sardines as above, then put them in a food processor or blender with 2 oz can anchovies in oil, drained, 1 crushed garlic clove, a sprig of parsley, and 2 tablespoons olive oil. Whizz to a paste, then spread over slices of toasted ciabatta, sprinkle with chopped parsley, and serve.

cod fillets with tomato & arugula

Serves **4**
Preparation time **5 minutes**
Cooking time **12–15 minutes**

4 chunky **cod fillets**, about
   5 oz each
3 tablespoons **olive oil**
2 **garlic cloves**, chopped
10 oz **cherry tomatoes on
   the vine**
2 tablespoons **balsamic
   vinegar**
4 tablespoons chopped **basil**
6 cups **arugula**
salt and **pepper**

Rub the cod fillets all over with 1 tablespoon of the oil and season well with salt and pepper. Scatter over the garlic and put the fish in a roasting pan lined with parchment paper. Arrange the cherry tomatoes alongside and drizzle with the remaining oil, the balsamic vinegar, and basil. Season with salt and pepper to taste.

Cook in a preheated oven, 425°F, for 12–15 minutes or until the fish is flaky and the tomatoes are roasted. Serve the cod with the tomatoes on a bed of arugula.

For cod with Italian-style salsa, oil and season the cod fillets as above and fry for 5–6 minutes or until cooked through and golden brown. To make the salsa, mix together 8 finely chopped sun-dried tomatoes, 2 tablespoons roughly chopped basil leaves, 1 tablespoon drained capers, 1 tablespoon lightly crushed toasted pine nuts, and 2 tablespoons olive oil in a bowl. Serve with an arugula salad.

smoked trout & grape salad

Serves **2**
Preparation time **15 minutes**

7 oz **smoked trout**
1 cup **red seedless grapes**
2 cups **watercress**
1 **fennel bulb**

Dressing
3 tablespoons **mayonnaise**
4 **cornichons**, finely diced
1½ tablespoons **capers**,
    drained and chopped
2 tablespoons **lemon juice**
salt and **pepper**

Flake the smoked trout into bite-sized pieces, removing any bones and skin, and place in a large salad bowl. Wash and drain the grapes and watercress leaves and add them to the bowl. Finely slice the fennel and stir through the salad.

Make the dressing. Mix together the mayonnaise, cornichons, capers, and lemon juice in a bowl. Season to taste with salt and pepper, then carefully mix through the salad and serve.

For crispy trout salad, prepare the dressing as above and add 1 finely chopped hard-boiled egg, 1 tablespoon chopped parsley, and 2 finely chopped anchovy fillets. Prepare the salad as above (omitting the smoked trout) and adding 1 green apple, cut into matchstick strips. Season 2 pieces of fresh trout, about 4½ oz each, with salt and pepper. Heat 1 tablespoon vegetable oil in a skillet over high heat and cook the trout, skin-side down, for 4 minutes, pressing it down with a metal spatula to give an evenly crispy skin. Turn the fish over and cook for a further 2 minutes or until it is just cooked through. Toss the salad with the dressing and serve immediately with the crispy trout.

salmon fillets with sage & quinoa

Serves **4**
Preparation time **5 minutes**
Cooking time **15 minutes**

1 cup **quinoa**
⅓ cup **butter**, at room
    temperature
8 **sage leaves**, chopped
small bunch of **chives**
grated zest and juice of
    1 **lemon**
4 **salmon fillets**, about
    6 oz each
1 tablespoon **olive oil**
salt and **pepper**

Cook the quinoa in a saucepan of unsalted boiling water for about 15 minutes or according to the package instructions until cooked but firm.

Meanwhile, mix together the butter, sage, chives, and lemon zest in a small bowl and season to taste with salt and pepper.

Rub the salmon fillets with the oil, season with pepper, and cook in a preheated skillet, turning carefully once, for about 8–10 minutes or until cooked through and the salmon flakes easily. Remove from the pan and leave to rest.

Drain the quinoa, stir in the lemon juice, and season to taste. Spoon onto serving plates, set a salmon fillet on each plate, and top each with a knob of sage butter.

For salmon with tarragon & couscous, replace the sage leaves with 4 sprigs of tarragon and the quinoa with 1⅓ cups couscous. Put the couscous in a large heatproof bowl and pour over 1⅔ cups boiling water. Cover and leave to stand for 5–8 minutes, or according to the package instructions, until the liquid has been absorbed and the grains are soft. Fluff up with a fork and season. Dress with a little lemon juice and olive oil and serve with the salmon, as above.

vegetables

flatbread pizzas with blue cheese

Serves **4**
Preparation time **5 minutes**
Cooking time **7–8 minutes**

4 x 8 inch **Mediterranean
   flatbreads**
7 oz **Gorgonzola** or **dolcelatte
   cheese**, crumbled
8 slices of **prosciutto**
2½ cups **arugula**
extra virgin olive oil, for
   drizzling
pepper

Put the flatbreads on 2 cookie sheets and scatter the centers with the blue cheese.

Bake in a preheated oven, 400°F, for 7–8 minutes or until the bases are crisp and the cheese has melted.

Top the pizzas with the prosciutto and arugula, season with pepper, and drizzle with oil. Serve immediately.

For naan pizzas, put 4 naan breads on 2 cookie sheets and spread 1 tablespoon purée over each one. Add 7 oz sliced mozzarella cheese and top with some drained mixed mushroom antipasto from a jar and a few thyme leaves. Bake as above until the cheese has melted.

ricotta & red onion tortillas

Serves **1**
Preparation time **10 minutes**
Cooking time **4–5 minutes**

3 tablespoons **ricotta cheese**
½ **red onion**, thinly sliced
1 **tomato**, finely chopped
¼ **green chili**, seeded and
   finely chopped
1 tablespoon chopped **fresh
   cilantro**
2 small **soft flour tortillas**
olive oil, for brushing

Mix together the ricotta, onion, tomato, chili, and cilantro in a bowl.

Heat a ridged griddle pan until hot. Brush the tortillas with a little oil, add to the pan, and cook very briefly on each side.

Spread half the ricotta mixture over one half of each tortilla and fold over the other half to cover. Serve immediately with a green salad.

For Mexican quesadillas, mix together ½ cored, seeded, and chopped red bell pepper, 1 finely sliced scallion, ¼ cup grated Cheddar cheese, 3 pieces of drained jalapeño pepper from a jar, and 1 tablespoon chopped fresh cilantro in a bowl. Spread the mixture on 1 tortilla and place the other tortilla on top. Place in a nonstick skillet and cook over medium heat until the cheese melts. Flip over and cook on the other side for a few more minutes. Slide onto a plate, cut into quarters, and serve with guacamole and sour cream.

fava bean & goat cheese salad

Serves **4**
Preparation time **10 minutes**
Cooking time **15–20 minutes**

½ pound **ripe tomatoes**
2 **garlic cloves**, peeled
5 tablespoons **extra virgin olive oil**
1 tablespoon good-quality **aged balsamic vinegar**
2 cups fresh or frozen **fava beans**
10 oz **dried farfalle**
7 oz **goat cheese**, crumbled
20 **basil leaves**, torn
salt and **pepper**

Put the tomatoes and garlic in a food processor or blender and whizz until the tomatoes are finely chopped. Tip into a large bowl and stir in the oil and vinegar. Season with salt and pepper.

Cook the fava beans in a saucepan of boiling water until tender (6–8 minutes for fresh fava beans or 2 minutes for frozen). Drain, refresh under cold running water, and drain again. Peel off the skins. Stir the beans into the tomato mixture and leave them to marinate while you cook the pasta.

Cook the pasta in a large saucepan of salted boiling water according to the package instructions until al dente. Drain, refresh under cold running water, and drain again.

Stir the pasta into the tomato and fava bean mixture. Add the goat cheese and basil, then toss gently. Season to taste with salt and pepper. Leave to stand for at least 5 minutes before serving.

For fresh soybean & pecorino farfalle salad, prepare the tomato and garlic mixture as above, replacing the fava beans with 1½ cups frozen or fresh soybeans, cooked for 3 minutes. Cook the pasta as above and stir into the soybean mixture. Omit the goat cheese and basil and stir in 2¼ oz shaved pecorino cheese and 3 tablespoons finely chopped mint or parsley.

vegetable & tofu stir-fry

Serves **4**
Preparation time **10 minutes**
Cooking time **7 minutes**

3 tablespoons **sunflower oil**
10 oz **firm tofu**, cubed
1 **onion**, sliced
2 **carrots**, sliced
1 cup **broccoli**, broken into
  small florets and stalks sliced
1 **red bell pepper**, cored,
  seeded, and sliced
1 large **zucchini**, sliced
1 ½ cups **sugar snap peas**
2 tablespoons **soy sauce**
2 tablespoons **sweet chili
  sauce**
½ cup **water**

To garnish
chopped **red chilies**
Thai or ordinary **basil leaves**

Heat 1 tablespoon of the oil in a wok or large skillet until starting to smoke, add the tofu, and stir-fry over high heat for 2 minutes or until golden. Remove with a slotted spoon and keep warm.

Heat the remaining oil in the pan, add the onion and carrots, and stir-fry for 1 ½ minutes. Add the broccoli and red bell pepper and stir-fry for 1 minute, then add the zucchini and sugar snap peas and stir-fry for 1 minute.

Mix together the soy and chili sauces and measurement water and add to the pan with the tofu. Cook for 1 minute. Serve in bowls, garnished with chopped red chilies and basil leaves.

For vegetable & cashew stir-fry, heat 1 tablespoon sunflower oil in a wok or large skillet, add 2 red chilies, seeded and sliced, 2 onions, cut into thin wedges, and ¼ teaspoon freshly ground black pepper and cook for 2 minutes. Add the vegetables as above and stir-fry until tender. Toss through 2 tablespoons soy sauce and 1 tablespoon sugar. Sprinkle with basil leaves and 1 ¼ cups toasted cashews. Serve immediately with jasmine rice.

corn & bell pepper frittata

Serves **4**
Preparation time **10 minutes**
Cooking time about **10 minutes**

2 tablespoons **olive oil**
4 **scallions**, thinly sliced
7 oz can **corn**, drained
5 oz bottled **roasted red bell peppers** in oil, drained and cut into strips
4 **eggs**, lightly beaten
1 cup sharp **Cheddar cheese**, grated
small handful of **chives**, finely chopped
salt and **pepper**

Heat the oil in a skillet with an ovenproof handle, add the scallions, corn, and red bell peppers, and cook for 30 seconds.

Add the eggs, Cheddar, chives, and salt and pepper to taste and cook over medium heat for 4–5 minutes or until the base is set.

Place the pan under a preheated hot broiler and cook the omelette for 3–4 minutes or until golden and set. Cut into wedges and serve immediately with a green salad and crusty bread.

For zucchini, pepper & Gruyère frittata, cook the scallion and red peppers as above, replacing the corn with 1½ cups finely chopped zucchini. Add the eggs, 1 cup grated Gruyère cheese (instead of the Cheddar) 4 tablespoons chopped mint (instead of the chives), season, and cook as above.

green curry with straw mushrooms

Serves **4**
Preparation time **10 minutes**
Cooking time **10 minutes**

1 ¼ cups **coconut milk**, plus
   extra for drizzling
1–2 tablespoons **green curry
   paste,** depending how hot
   you prefer it
1 ¼ cups **vegetable stock**
2 **eggplant**, roughly chopped
   into large chunks
3 tablespoons **soft brown
   sugar**
4 teaspoons **soy sauce**
1 oz **fresh ginger root**, peeled
   and finely chopped
14 oz can **straw mushrooms**,
   drained
1 small **green bell pepper**,
   cored, seeded, and thinly
   sliced
salt

Put the coconut milk and curry paste in a saucepan over medium heat and stir well. Pour in the stock, then add the eggplant, sugar, soy sauce, ginger, and salt to taste.

Bring to a boil and cook, stirring, for 5 minutes. Add the mushrooms and chopped green pepper, reduce the heat, and cook for 2 minutes until piping hot.

Serve in bowls, drizzled with a little extra coconut milk.

For vegetable korma, heat 1 tablespoon vegetable oil in a large saucepan, add 1 finely diced onion, 3 bruised cardamom pods, 2 teaspoons each of ground cumin and ground coriander seed and ½ teaspoon turmeric and cook over low heat for 5–6 minutes or until the onion is light golden. Add 1 seeded and chopped green chili, 1 crushed garlic clove, and a thumb-sized piece of fresh ginger root, peeled and grated, and cook for 1 minute, then add a selection of 14 oz prepared mixed vegetables, such as cauliflower, bell peppers, carrots, and zucchini, and cook for a further 5 minutes. Remove the pan from the heat and stir through ¾ cup yogurt and 2 tablespoons ground almonds. Serve sprinkled with chopped cilantro, accompanied with basmati rice.

panzanella salad

Serves **4**
Preparation time **15 minutes**,
   plus standing

1 ¼ lb large **tomatoes**
1 tablespoon **sea salt**
8 inch **ciabatta loaf**
½ **red onion**, finely chopped
handful of **basil leaves**, plus
   extra to garnish
1 tablespoon **red wine
   vinegar**
2 tablespoons **olive oil**
12 pickled **white anchovies**,
   drained
salt and **pepper**

Roughly chop the tomatoes into ¾ inch pieces and put
them in a nonmetallic bowl. Sprinkle over the sea salt
and leave to stand for 1 hour.

Remove the crust from the ciabatta and tear the bread
into rough chunks.

Give the tomatoes a good squash with clean hands,
then add the bread, onion, basil, vinegar, and oil. Season
to taste with salt and pepper. Mix together carefully
and transfer to serving plates. Garnish with the drained
anchovies and basil leaves and serve.

For tomato & bean salad, finely slice 1 red onion,
cover with 4 tablespoons red wine vinegar and leave
to stand for about 30 minutes. Cut an 8 inch ciabatta
loaf into chunks and place in a roasting pan. Drizzle with
olive oil, season with salt and pepper, and add 2 sprigs
of thyme. Cook the ciabatta in a preheated oven, 375°F,
for 8 minutes or until golden and crispy. Dice 10 oz
tomatoes and put them in a large bowl. Add a drained
13 oz can borlotti beans, a drained 13 oz can cannellini
beans and 1 bunch of chopped basil. Remove the onion
from the vinegar, reserving the vinegar, and add to the
salad with 12 drained pickled white anchovies. Add
1 teaspoon Dijon mustard to the reserved vinegar and
whisk in 5 tablespoons olive oil. Season with salt and
pepper. Add the dressing to the salad, toss thoroughly,
and serve garnished with the ciabatta croûtons.

curried couscous salad

Serves **4**
Preparation time **15 minutes**

juice of **1 orange**
2 teaspoons **mild curry paste**
1 ¼ cups **couscous**
½ cup **golden raisins**
1 ¼ cups **boiling water**
8 oz **smoked mackerel fillets**
1 small **red onion**, finely
   chopped
½ **red bell pepper**, cored,
   seeded, and diced
2 **tomatoes**, chopped
small bunch of **fresh cilantro**,
   roughly chopped
pepper

Put the orange juice and curry paste into a heatproof bowl and stir together. Add the couscous, golden raisins, and a little pepper, then pour over the boiling water and fork together. Cover and leave to stand for 5 minutes or according to the package instructions until the liquid has been absorbed.

Meanwhile, peel the skin off the mackerel fillets and break the flesh into large flakes, discarding any bones.

Add the mackerel, onion, red bell pepper, and tomatoes to the couscous and fork together lightly. Sprinkle the chopped cilantro over the top, spoon onto plates, and serve immediately.

For curried couscous salad with lamb cutlets, mix together 4 tablespoons plain yogurt and 1 teaspoon mild curry paste in a nonmetallic dish. Add 12 lamb cutlets and coat evenly in the mixture. Prepare the couscous salad as above, omitting the mackerel. Heat 2 tablespoons vegetable oil in a large griddle pan over high heat, add the lamb, and fry for 3 minutes on each side or until cooked through. Serve the lamb on the couscous salad, garnished with chopped cilantro.

red bell pepper & cheese tortellini

Serves **4**
Preparation time **10 minutes**,
  plus cooling
Cooking time **15 minutes**

2 **red bell peppers**
2 **garlic cloves**, chopped
8 **scallions**, finely sliced
1 lb **fresh cheese-stuffed
  tortellini** or any other fresh
  stuffed tortellini
¾ cup **olive oil**
2 tablespoons **Parmesan
  cheese**, finely grated
salt and **pepper**

Cut the bell peppers into large pieces, removing the cores and seeds. Lay skin-side up on a broiler rack and cook under a preheated broiler until the skin blackens and blisters. Transfer to a plastic bag, tie the top to enclose, and leave to cool. Then peel away the skin.

Place the bell peppers and garlic in a food processor or blender and blend until fairly smooth. Stir in the scallions and set aside.

Cook the tortellini in a large saucepan of boiling water according to the package instructions until al dente. Drain and return to the pan.

Stir the bell pepper mixture into the pasta, add the oil and Parmesan, and toss together. Season to taste with salt and pepper and serve immediately.

For warm ham & red bell pepper tortellini salad, broil and peel the red bell peppers as above, then thinly slice the flesh. While the tortellini is cooking, thinly slice 1 red onion. Drain the pasta and toss with 4 oz chopped cooked ham, 4 cups arugula, and the onion and red peppers. Serve immediately.

mushroom stroganoff

Serves **4**

Preparation time **10 minutes**

Cooking time **10 minutes**

1 tablespoon **butter**

2 tablespoons **olive oil**

1 **onion,** thinly sliced

4 **garlic cloves,** finely chopped

1 lb **chestnut mushrooms,** sliced

2 tablespoons **wholegrain mustard**

1 cup **crème fraîche**

salt and **pepper**

3 tablespoons chopped **parsley,** to garnish

Heat the butter and oil in a large skillet, add the onion and garlic, and fry gently until softened and beginning to brown.

Add the mushrooms to the skillet and cook until softened and beginning to brown. Stir in the mustard and crème fraîche and just heat through. Season to taste with salt and pepper, then serve immediately, garnished with the chopped parsley.

For mushroom soup with garlic croûtons, cook the mushrooms as above. Remove the crusts from 2 thick slices of day-old white bread and rub with 2 halved garlic cloves. Cut the bread into cubes. Fry the cubes of bread in a shallow depth of vegetable oil in a skillet, turning continuously, for 5 minutes or until browned all over and crisp. Drain on paper towels. After adding the mustard and crème fraîche to the mushroom mixture as above, add 1¾ cups boiling vegetable stock, then purée the mixture in a food processor or blender until smooth. Serve in warmed bowls, topped with the croûtons and garnished with the chopped parsley.

cheesy polenta & mushrooms

Serves **4**
Preparation time **10 minutes**
Cooking time **15 minutes**

13 oz **mixed wild mushrooms,** such as **porcini, girolles** and **chanterelles**
2 tablespoons **butter**
2 **garlic cloves**, chopped
5 whole **sage leaves**
¼ cup **dry vermouth**
salt and pepper

Polenta
3 cups **water**
7 oz **instant polenta**
2 oz **Parmesan cheese**, freshly grated
¼ cup **butter**, cubed

Brush away any soil and grit from the mushrooms with a moist cloth, then slice the porcini and tear any other large mushrooms in half. Set aside.

Melt the butter in a large skillet over medium-high heat. Add the garlic, sage, and the dense, tougher mushrooms and cook for 2–3 minutes. Add the remaining mushrooms, season with salt and pepper, and cook for 2–3 minutes until soft and cooked through. Pour in the vermouth and cook, stirring, for 1 minute.

For the polenta, bring the measurement water to the boil in a large, heavy-based saucepan. Put the polenta in a large measuring cup and pour into the water in a slow but steady stream, stirring vigorously with a wooden spoon to stop any lumps from forming. Reduce the heat to a slow simmer and cook, stirring frequently, for about 5 minutes, or until the polenta is thick and comes away from the side of the pan. Stir in the butter and season with salt and pepper.

Divide the polenta between 4 serving plates, then top with the mushrooms.

For cheesy polenta with mushrooms & tomato, cook the mushrooms as above, but replace the rosemary with 3 chopped thyme sprigs and use ⅔ cup full-bodied red wine instead of the vermouth. When the wine has boiled for 1 minute, stir in 1¼ cups tomato purée. Season with salt and pepper and bring to a boil, then simmer for 5 minutes. Cook the polenta as above, then gradually stir in the cheese. Serve with the mushroom and tomato mixture.

spring garden pasta salad

Serves **4**

Preparation time **10 minutes**, plus cooling

Cooking time **10 minutes**

4 tablespoons **extra virgin olive oil**

1 **garlic clove**, crushed

finely grated zest and juice of ½ **lemon**

6 **scallions**, thinly sliced

6 oz **dried fusilli**

5 oz **asparagus spears**, cut into 1 inch pieces

1½ cups **green beans**, trimmed and cut into 1 inch pieces

⅓ cup fresh or frozen **peas**

1 **buffalo mozzarella cheese ball**, drained and torn into small pieces

2 cups **watercress**

2 tablespoons roughly chopped **parsley**

2 tablespoons snipped **chives**

8 **basil leaves**, torn

salt and **pepper**

Mix the oil, garlic, lemon zest and juice, and scallions together in a large, nonmetallic serving bowl and leave to infuse while you cook the pasta.

Cook the pasta in a large saucepan of salted boiling water according to the package instructions until al dente, adding the asparagus, beans, and peas 3 minutes before the end of the cooking time.

Drain the pasta and vegetables lightly, then stir into the prepared dressing. Set aside in a cool place until cooled to room temperature.

Stir the remaining ingredients into the pasta salad. Season with salt and pepper, then leave the dish to stand for at least 5 minutes for the flavors to mingle before serving.

For sugar snap pea & fava bean salad, make the dressing and cook the pasta as above, replacing the asparagus tips with 2 cups sugar snap peas and the green beans with 1 cup fava beans. Slice the sugar snap peas in half and add them, together with the beans, to the pan 3–5 minutes before the end of the pasta cooking time. Replace the watercress with 2 cups of arugula.

mango curry

Serves **4**
Preparation time **10 minutes**
Cooking time **8–10 minutes**

1 tablespoon **vegetable oil**
1 teaspoon **mustard seeds**
1 **onion**, halved and thinly sliced
15–20 **curry leaves**, fresh or dried
½ teaspoon **dried red chili flakes**
1 teaspoon peeled and grated **fresh ginger root**
1 **green chili**, seeded and sliced
1 teaspoon **ground turmeric**
3 ripe **mangoes**, peeled, stoned and thinly sliced
1⅔ cups **plain yogurt**, lightly beaten
salt

Heat the oil in a large saucepan until hot, add the mustard seeds, onion, curry leaves, and chili flakes and fry, stirring, for 4–5 minutes or until the onion is lightly browned.

Add the ginger and chili and stir-fry for 1 minute, then add the turmeric and stir to mix well.

Remove the pan from the heat, add the mangoes and yogurt, and stir continuously until well mixed. Season to taste with salt.

Return the pan to low heat and heat through for 1 minute, stirring continuously. (Do not let it boil or the curry will curdle.) Serve immediately with 4 warm chapattis.

For eggplant & pea curry, heat 3 tablespoons sunflower oil in a large skillet until hot, then add 4 peeled and cubed medium-sized potatoes, 1 eggplant, cut into small chunks, 1 cup frozen peas, 2 finely sliced onions, 2 crushed garlic cloves, 1 tablespoon ginger paste and 2 tablespoons medium curry powder. Stir-fry for 3–4 minutes or until the onion has softened and is turning golden, then pour in 2½ cups chicken or vegetable stock and cook for 10–15 minutes or until the stock has reduced. Stir in ⅔ cup crème fraîche and serve with naan bread.

asparagus & taleggio pizza

Serves **2**
Preparation time **5 minutes**
Cooking time **10 minutes**

5 tablespoons **tomato purée**
1 tablespoon **red pesto**
pinch of **salt**
1 large ready-made **garlic pizza bread**
8 oz **Taleggio cheese**, rind removed and discarded, cheese sliced
1¾ cups **cherry tomatoes**, halved
6 oz **fine asparagus spears**, trimmed
2 tablespoons **olive oil**
pepper
a few **basil** leaves

Mix together the tomato purée, pesto, and salt in a small bowl and spread the mixture over the top of the garlic pizza bread. Top with the Taleggio, cherry tomatoes, and asparagus spears and drizzle with the oil.

Bake the pizza directly on the oven rack or on a pizza pan at the top of a preheated oven, 400°F, for 10 minutes or until the asparagus is tender and the pizza base is crisp. Grind some pepper over the top and scatter over basil leaves before serving.

For artichoke, egg & Parma ham pizza, omit the red pesto and spread the tomato purée and salt over the pizza bread as above, then top with a 13 oz can artichoke hearts, drained and quartered, 8 slices of Parma ham torn into shreds, and 3 handfuls of chopped pitted black olives. Break a small egg into the center of the pizza, then top with 8 oz mozzarella torn into pieces and some basil leaves. Bake as above.

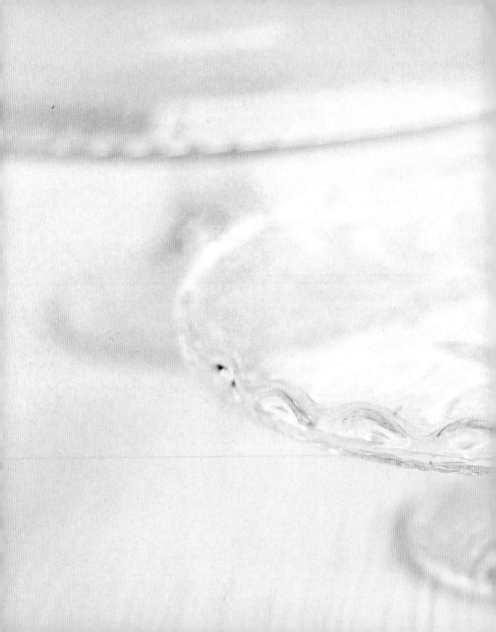

sweet treats

heavenly chocolate puddings

Serves **4**
Preparation time **10 minutes**
Cooking time **10 minutes**

3½ oz **milk chocolate**,
 broken up
¼ cup **unsalted butter**
⅓ cup **cocoa powder**
⅓ cup **golden superfine
 sugar**
2 **eggs**, separated
1 teaspoon **vanilla extract**
4 tablespoons **light cream**
confectioners' sugar, for
 dusting

Melt the chocolate and butter in a large heatproof mixing bowl placed over a pan of barely simmering water, making sure the surface of the water does not touch the bowl. Remove from the heat, add the cocoa powder, **two-thirds** of the sugar, the egg yolks, vanilla extract, and cream and beat the mixture to a smooth paste.

Whisk the egg whites in a clean bowl until peaking and gradually whisk in the remaining sugar. Use a large metal spoon to fold one-quarter of the meringue into the chocolate mixture to lighten it, then fold in the remainder.

Spoon the mixture into 4 small ramekin dishes or similar-sized ovenproof dishes. Bake in a preheated oven, 325°F, for 8–10 minutes or until a very thin crust has formed over the surface. Dust with confectioners' sugar and serve immediately.

For boozy chocolate puddings, stir 2 tablespoons brandy, rum, or orange liqueur into the mixture with the cream. Continue as above.

cherry & cinnamon zabaglione

Serves **4**
Preparation time **10 minutes**
Cooking time about
12 minutes

4 **egg yolks**
½ cup **superfine sugar**
⅔ cup **cream sherry**
large pinch of **ground
cinnamon**, plus extra to
decorate
13 oz can **black cherries in
syrup**

Pour 2 inches water into a medium-sized saucepan and bring to a boil. Set a large heatproof bowl over the pan, making sure that the water does not touch the base of the bowl. Reduce the heat so that the water is simmering, then add the egg yolks, sugar, sherry, and cinnamon to the bowl. Whisk for 5–8 minutes or until very thick and foamy and the custard leaves a trail when the whisk is lifted above the mixture.

Drain off some of the cherry syrup and then tip the cherries and just a little of the syrup into a small saucepan. Warm through, then spoon into 4 glasses. Pour the warm zabaglione over the top and serve dusted with cinnamon and with amaretti.

For raspberry zabaglione, put 1¾ cups raspberries, reserving 12 for decoration, in a food processor or blender with a squeeze of lemon juice and blitz to a purée. Push through a sieve to remove the seeds and set aside. Make the zabaglione as above and when ready pour into 4 glasses. Swirl through the raspberry purée to create a ripple effect and decorate with the reserved raspberries. Serve with biscotti.

spiced bananas

Serves **8**
Preparation time **10 minutes**
Cooking time **10 minutes**

8 **bananas**, peeled
2 tablespoons **lemon juice**
8 tablespoons **light muscovado sugar**
¼ cup **butter**, softened
1 teaspoon **cinnamon**

Rum mascarpone cream
8 oz **mascarpone cheese**
2 tablespoons **rum**
1–2 tablespoons **granulated sugar**

Put each banana on a double piece of foil. Drizzle over the lemon juice and sprinkle 1 tablespoon of the brown sugar on each banana.

Beat together the butter and cinnamon in a bowl until creamy, then spoon over the bananas. Wrap each banana tightly in the foil and cook over a barbecue or under a preheated medium-hot broiler for 10 minutes.

Meanwhile, make the rum mascarpone cream. Mix together the mascarpone, rum, and sugar in a bowl.

Unwrap the bananas and slice thickly. Serve immediately with the rum mascarpone cream.

For BBQ pineapple with rum butter glaze, cut off the top and base of 1 large fresh pineapple and slice off the skin, then cut into quarters and remove the core from each quarter. Slice the quarters across into 1 inch thick triangular slices. Sprinkle both sides with a little superfine sugar and cook on a barbecue for 5–6 minutes or until lightly caramelized. Meanwhile, melt ⅓ cup butter in a small pan, then add ⅓ cup Demerara sugar and the juice of ½ lime. Scrape out the seeds of 1 vanilla pod and add to the pan with 2 tablespoons dark rum. Stir until the mixture has melted and bubbled to form a smooth glaze. Place the pineapple slices on a plate, spoon over the rum butter, and serve immediately with ice cream.

italian trifle

Serves **4**

Preparation **10 minutes**, plus cooling and chilling

Cooking time **10 minutes**

8 **ladyfingers**

2 tablespoons **blueberry jam**

¼ cup **sweet sherry** or **sweet white wine**

1⅔ cups **blueberries**

1¼ cups **milk**

1 tablespoon **cornstarch**

2 **egg yolks**

2 tablespoons **superfine sugar**

1¼ cups **whipping cream**

2 oz **dark chocolate**, grated

Spread the ladyfingers with the blueberry jam and put in a glass bowl. Sprinkle over the sherry or white wine and half of the blueberries.

Mix a little of the milk with the cornstarch until smooth. Stir into the rest of the milk. Pour into a saucepan and bring to a boil, stirring continuously as the milk thickens. When it is boiling and smooth, remove the pan from the heat.

Whisk the egg yolks and sugar in a bowl until light and creamy. Add the milk slowly, whisking all the time. Mix well, pour over the blueberries and ladyfingers, then sprinkle the rest of the blueberries over the top. Leave to cool, then chill, preferably overnight.

When ready to serve, whip the cream until soft peaks form and spread it over the trifle. Sprinkle the grated chocolate over the top.

For fresh citrus trifle, mix together the juice of 3 oranges and ⅓ cup limoncello in a bowl. Put the ladyfingers in a glass bowl and pour over the orange mixture. Make the custard mixture as above, pour over the sponge, and leave to cool. Chill as above. When ready to serve, spread with the whipped cream and decorate with 1 cupraspberries and shavings of dark chocolate.

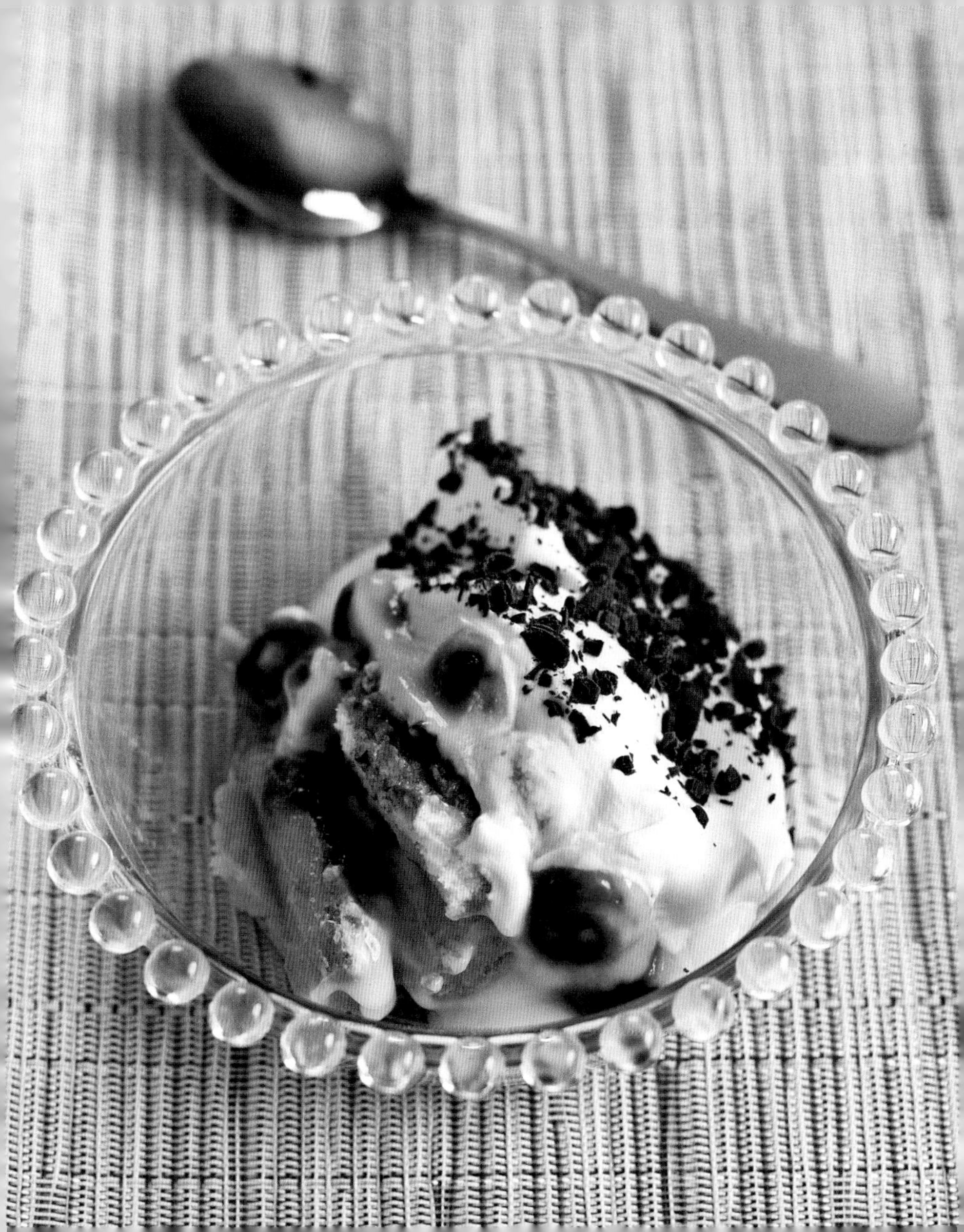

pancake stack with maple syrup

Serves **4**
Preparation time **10 minutes**
Cooking time **6 minutes**

1 **egg**
¾ cup **all-purpose flour**
½ cup **milk**
2½ tablespoons **vegetable oil**
1 tablespoon **superfine sugar**
maple syrup, for drizzling

Put the egg, flour, milk, oil, and sugar in a food processor or blender and blend until the mixture is smooth and creamy.

Heat a large nonstick skillet over medium heat and put in 4 half-ladlefuls of the batter to make 4 pancakes. After about 1 minute the tops of the pancakes will start to set and air bubbles will rise to the top and burst. Use a spatula to turn the pancakes over and cook on the other side for 1 minute. Repeat twice more until you have used all the batter and made 12 small pancakes in total.

Bring the pancakes to the table as a stack, drizzled with maple syrup, and serve 3 pancakes to each person, with scoops of ice cream.

For orange-flavored pancakes, make a batter as above but with 1 cup all-purpose flour, 2 teaspoons each superfine sugar and grated orange zest, 1 teaspoon each cream of tartar and corn syrup, ½ teaspoon each salt and baking soda, 1 egg, ½ cup warm milk and a few drops of orange essence. Cook the pancakes as above.

passionfruit yogurt fool

Serves **4**
Preparation time **8 minutes**

6 **passionfruit**
1 ¼ cups **Greek-style yogurt**
1 tablespoon **liquid honey**
¾ cup **whipping cream**
4 **shortbread cookies**,
   to serve

Halve the passionfruit and remove the flesh and seeds. Put the yogurt in a bowl, then stir in the flesh and seeds with the honey.

Whip the cream until soft peaks form, then fold into the yogurt mixture.

Spoon into tall glasses and serve each with a shortbread cookie.

For mango & lime yogurt fool, omit the passionfruit, instead puréeing 1 large ripe peeled and seeded mango with the grated zest of 1 lime and confectioners' sugar to taste. Mix into the yogurt, omitting the honey, and fold in the whipped cream.

warm, nutty chocolate fondue

Serves **4**
Preparation time **15 minutes**
Cooking time **10 minutes**

3½ oz **bar Toblerone
chocolate**
2 oz **dark chocolate**
1 tablespoon **rum**
2 tablespoons **heavy cream**

To serve
selection of **fruit**, such as
strawberries, cherries, and
sliced banana
cookies

Melt the Toblerone and dark chocolate in a heatproof bowl set over a saucepan of gently simmering water. When melted, add the rum and cream, and continue to heat, stirring, for 1 minute.

Pour the chocolate mixture into a fondue pot and keep warm on a burner. Dip a selection of fruits and cookies into the chocolate and enjoy.

For butterscotch fondue, melt ½ cup soft light brown sugar, 4 tablespoons vanilla superfine sugar, ¾ cup corn syrup and ¼ cup unsalted butter in a saucepan, then boil for 5 minutes. Add 1 cup heavy cream and ½ teaspoon vanilla extract and stir together, then remove the pan from the heat. Pour into a fondue pot and serve with fruit as above.

pears with minted mascarpone

Serves **4**
Preparation time **10 minutes**
Cooking time **5 minutes**

2 tablespoons **unsalted butter**
2 tablespoons **liquid honey**
4 ripe **pears**, such as Bartlett or Comice, cored and quartered lengthways
lemon juice, for sprinkling

Minted mascarpone
1 tablespoon finely chopped **mint**
1 tablespoon **granulated sugar**
6 oz **mascarpone cheese**

To decorate
mint sprigs
sifted **confectioners' sugar**
ground cinnamon

Melt the butter in a small saucepan. Remove the pan from the heat and stir in the honey.

Sprinkle the pear slices with a little lemon juice as soon as they are cut to prevent them from discoloring. Line a baking pan with foil and lay the pear slices on it. Brush the pears with the butter and honey mixture and cook under a preheated broiler on its highest setting for 5 minutes.

Meanwhile, make the minted mascarpone. Lightly whisk the mint and granulated sugar into the mascarpone in a bowl.

Arrange the pear slices on 4 plates and top each with a spoonful of the minted mascarpone. Decorate with mint sprigs, then lightly dust with confectioners' sugar and cinnamon and serve immediately.

For pear & jam tarts, lay out a 10 oz package of ready-rolled puff pastry, thawed if frozen, on a floured surface and cut out 4 circles using a 7 inch plate as a template. Transfer the circles to 2 buttered cookie sheets. Peel, core, and finely slice the pears and place in a bowl. Toss with just enough superfine sugar to coat the fruit and 2 tablespoons freshly squeezed orange juice. Place 1 tablespoon any flavored jam in the middle of each pastry circle, fan out the fruit slices on top, and fold in the sides of the pastry to hold it all together. Bake in a preheated oven, 425°F, for 10–12 minutes until the fruit has softened and the pastry is crisp and golden. Serve with vanilla ice cream.

pain perdu with mixed berries

Serves **4**
Preparation time **10 minutes**
Cooking time **10 minutes**

4 thick slices of **brioche**
2 **eggs**
6 tablespoons **milk**
¼ cup **unsalted butter**
⅔ cup **Greek-style yogurt**
2 cups **raspberries**
⅔ cup **blueberries**
confectioners' sugar, for
    dusting, or **maple syrup**, for
    drizzling

Cut each slice of brioche into 2 triangles. Beat the eggs and milk in a shallow bowl with a fork.

Heat half the butter in a large skillet. Quickly dip the bread, a triangle at a time, into the egg mixture, then put as many as you can get into the skillet. Cook on medium heat until the underside is golden. Turn over and cook the second side, then remove from the skillet and keep warm. Heat the remaining butter in the skillet and dip and cook the remaining brioche triangles.

Transfer the cooked triangles to 4 serving plates, top with spoonfuls of yogurt, a scattering of berries, and a light dusting of sifted confectioners' sugar or a drizzle of maple syrup. Serve immediately.

For spiced pain perdu with apricots, simmer 1 cup ready-to-eat dried apricots with the juice of 1 orange and ½ cup water for 10 minutes or until tender. Cut 4 slices of fruit bread in half. Beat the egg and milk as above with ¼ teaspoon ground cinnamon, then dip and fry the fruit bread as above. Arrange on plates with spoonfuls of Greek-style yogurt and the warm apricot compôte.

sweet chestnut mess

Serves **4**
Preparation time **15 minutes**

1 cup **fromage blanc**
1 tablespoon **confectioners' sugar**, sifted
⅓ cup **sweetened chestnut purée**
3½ oz **meringues**, crushed
dark chocolate shards, to decorate

Beat together the fromage blanc and confectioners' sugar in a large bowl. Stir in half the chestnut purée and the crushed meringues.

Spoon the remaining chestnut purée into 4 individual serving dishes and top with the meringue mess. Decorate with the chocolate shards and serve.

For sweet chestnut pancakes, stir all the chestnut purée into the fromage blanc. Heat 8 ready-made pancakes according to the package instructions and spread them with the chestnut purée mixture. Roll them up and dust with cocoa powder and confectioners' sugar.

caramelized blueberry custards

Serves **6**
Preparation time **10 minutes**,
  plus cooling
Cooking time **5 minutes**

²/₃ cup **granulated sugar**
3 tablespoons **cold water**
2 tablespoons **boiling water**
1 cup fresh (not frozen)
  blueberries
1²/₃ cups **fromage blanc**
14 oz can or carton **custard**

Put the sugar and measurement cold water into a skillet and heat gently, stirring very occasionally, until the sugar has completely dissolved. Bring to a boil, then cook for 3–4 minutes, without stirring, until the syrup is just changing color and is golden around the edges.

Add the measurement boiling water, standing well back because the syrup will spit, then tilt the skillet to mix. Add the blueberries and cook for 1 minute. Remove the skillet from the heat and leave to cool slightly.

Mix the fromage blanc and custard together, spoon into 6 small dishes, then spoon the blueberry mixture over the top. Serve immediately with baby meringues, if liked.

For banana custards, make the caramel as above, then add 2 sliced bananas instead of the blueberries. Cool slightly, then spoon over the custard and fromage blanc mixture. Decorate with grated dark chocolate.

tiramisu with raspberry surprise

Serves **4**

Preparation time **15 minutes**, plus chilling

6 tablespoons very strong **espresso coffee**

3 tablespoons **grappa** or **brandy**

16 **ladyfingers**

6 oz **mascarpone cheese**

2 **eggs**, separated

½ cup **confectioners' sugar**

1½ cups **raspberries**

1 oz **dark chocolate**

Stir together the coffee and grappa or brandy in a bowl. Dip the ladyfingers into the liquid to coat evenly, then arrange half of them in the base of a small shallow dish or serving platter, pouring over any excess liquid.

Whisk together the mascarpone, egg yolks, and confectioners' sugar in a bowl until smooth and well blended. In a separate clean bowl, whisk the egg whites until stiff and glossy, then fold the egg whites and the mascarpone mixture together until well blended.

Spoon half the mixture over the soaked ladyfingers and smooth the surface. Scatter half the raspberries over the top. Repeat with another layer of ladyfingers, followed by the rest of the marscarpone mixture and finish with the remaining raspberries on top. Grate the chocolate straight onto the mixture. Cover and chill, preferably overnight, until set.

For winter gold tiramisu, replace the grappa or brandy with 2 tablespoons Grand Marnier, and the raspberries with the juice of 1 large orange. When whisking the mascarpone with the egg yolks and confectioners' sugar, add the grated zest of 1 orange. Continue as above, replacing the dark chocolate with a spicy, orange-flavored dark chocolate.

almond brittle

Serves **8**

Preparation time **5 minutes**,
   plus cooling

Cooking time **10 minutes**

1¾ cups **blanched almonds**
1 cup **sugar**
4 tablespoons **water**

Line a baking pan with nonstick parchment paper.

Put the almonds on a broiler pan and toast under a preheated broiler until lightly brown. Leave to cool slightly, then roughly chop.

Heat a nonstick skillet over low heat, add the sugar and measurement water, and dissolve, without stirring, until it has melted and turned golden brown. Be careful that the heat is not too high or the caramel will burn and have a very bitter taste.

Stir in the almonds, then pour the mixture onto the prepared baking pan. Leave to cool, then break into small pieces and store in an airtight container until required. Serve with ice cream or good strong coffee.

For French almond mendiants, melt 7 oz dark chocolate in a heatproof bowl set over a saucepan of gently simmering water. Spoon teaspoonfuls of the melted mixture onto a baking pan lined with nonstick parchment paper. Using the back of a spoon, shape into small disks, then sprinkle each disk with a few blanched almonds and some dried fruits. Leave to set in a cool place (ideally, not a refrigerator) before serving.

spiced infused fruit salad

Serves **6**
Preparation time **15 minutes**
Cooking time **5 minutes**

1 **vanilla pod**
¾ cup **water**
2½ tablespoons **superfine sugar**
1 small **hot red chili**, halved lengthways and seeded
4 **clementines**
2 **peaches**
½ **cantaloupe**, seeded
½ cup **blueberries**

Use the tip of a small, sharp knife to score the vanilla pod lengthways through to the center. Put the measurement water and sugar in a saucepan and heat gently until the sugar has dissolved. Add the vanilla pod and chili and heat gently for a further 2 minutes. Remove the pan from the heat and leave to cool while you prepare the fruit.

Remove the peel from the clementines and slice the flesh. Stone and slice the peaches. Cut the cantaloupe flesh into small chunks, peeling and discarding the skin.

Put the prepared fruit and blueberries into a serving dish and mix together, then pour over the warm syrup, Serve immediately decorated with the chili and half a vanilla pod (discard just before eating), or cover and chill until ready to serve.

For classic Italian fruit salad, mix together 2 cups good-quality, freshly squeezed orange juice and the grated zest of 1 lemon in a large bowl. Halve, stone, and slice 2 peaches, peel, core, and slice 1 pear and seed and slice ½ small melon, discarding the skin, and add to the bowl with 1 cup halved seedless red grapes. Stir in 3 tablespoons cherry liqueur and 3 tablespoons superfine sugar, then chill until ready to serve.

banana lassi

Serves **4**
Preparation time **10 minutes**

3 ripe **bananas**, roughly
  chopped
2 cups **plain yogurt**
1 cup **cold water**
1–2 tablespoons **superfine
  sugar**
¼ teaspoon ground
  cardamom seeds, plus extra
  for decorating (optional)

Put all the ingredients in a food processor or blender and blend until smooth.

Pour into tall glasses and serve chilled, decorated with extra cardamom seeds if liked. This makes an ideal breakfast drink.

For a summer berry lassi, use only 1 banana, replace the cold water with 1 cup apple juice, omit the cardamom and add 1½ cups raspberries and 1⅓ cups blackberries.

affogato al caffe

Serves **4**
Preparation time **10 minutes**

8 scoops of **low-fat vanilla
  ice cream**
4 freshly made **espresso
  coffees**

Put 2 scoops of ice cream in each of 4 cappuccino cups or dessert bowls.

Pour a freshly made espresso coffee over each cup or bowl and serve immediately with biscotti, if liked.

For affogato al mocha, replace the vanilla ice cream with 8 scoops of rich, dark chocolate ice cream, pour over the coffee as above and top with ½ cup finely chopped dark chocolate.

index

acknowledgments

Executive editor: Eleanor Maxfield
Text editor: Jo Murray
Art direction and design: Penny Stock
Photographer: Stephen Conroy
Home economist: Sara Lewis
Stylist: Liz Hippisley
Production: Caroline Alberti

Photography copyright © Octopus Publishing Group Limited/Stephen Conroy, except the following: copyright © Octopus Publishing Group/Will Heap 11 bottom, 14, 119, 133, 202, 221, 225; /Sandra Lane 53; /William Lingwood 189; /David Munns 51, 69, 78, 100, 125; /Lis Parsons 9 top, 10 bottom, 16, 57, 59, 61, 75, 83, 87, 93, 169, 172, 179, 187, 197; /Gareth Sambidge 159, 213; /William Shaw 15 bottom; /Ian Wallace 8, 15 top, 27, 29, 33, 39, 41, 95, 137, 161, 181.